Published for the
Indiana University English Curriculum Study Center
EDWARD B. JENKINSON, *Director*

PREVIOUSLY PUBLISHED

On Teaching Literature:
Essays for Secondary School Teachers

Teaching Literature in Grades Seven through Nine

Two Approaches to Teaching Syntax

On Teaching the Bible as Literature: A Guide to
Selected Biblical Narratives for Secondary Schools

What is Language? And Other Teaching Units
for Grades Seven through Twelve

Teaching Literature in Grades Ten through Twelve

Books for Teachers of English:
An Annotated Bibliography

Writing as a Process of Discovery: Some Structured
Theme Assignments for Grades Five through Twelve

FORTHCOMING

Essays on Teaching Speech in the High School

On Teaching the Old Testament as Literature

On Teaching Speech in Elementary and Junior High Schools

EDITED BY

J. JEFFERY AUER

Chairman and Professor of Speech and Theatre
Indiana University

and

EDWARD B. JENKINSON

Associate Professor of Education
Coordinator for School English Language Arts
Director, Indiana University English
Curriculum Study Center

BLOOMINGTON   *Indiana University Press*   LONDON

Published in Canada by Fitzhenry & Whiteside Limited,
Don Mills, Ontario

Library of Congress catalog card number: 73–138412

ISBN: 0–253–34240–6

Manufactured in the United States of America

CONTENTS

INTRODUCTION

In school libraries we are notoriously unsubtle: the largest sign in sight shouts "No Talking!" Though less blatantly promulgated, essentially the same rule governs most elementary school classrooms. "Even in the most supposedly enlightened schools," reports John Holt in *How Children Learn*, "the usual rule in almost every class is that a child talks only to the teacher, and then only when called on. . . . After school children head for home, where their time is likely to be taken up with homework and TV, and where in any case nobody else may be very interested in talking to them. The result of this kind of education is that children of ten or even older may be no better at talking than they were at five." At the Anglo-American Seminar on the Teaching of English, held at Dartmouth College in the late summer of 1966, James Moffett voiced a similar complaint: "Most of the furious flagging of hands and clamorous talking at once in traditional classes is actually provoked by the teacher, who usually has asked a question to which he knows the answer. The children are competitively bidding for the teacher's approval and place no value on what other children are saying." In short, though the children need the practice in talking, the teacher does most of it, and what he does not do, he directs.

The plain fact of the matter is that no one, at home or at school, much cares about teaching young children anything about the creativity or even the utility of oral discourse. To be sure, when an infant first says anything that resembles a word, his parents are elated, but after he has acquired a basic child's vocabulary and has begun to demonstrate some sentence sense, the novelty wears off for even doting parents. Indeed, when he talks and questions too much, he is apt to get shoved in front of the electronic pacifier, and the television pitchman becomes a surrogate parent—and a model for his own speech behavior.

Then the child leaves home for school, his speech communication habits essentially untaught but "caught" from the circumscribed conversation at home, the untutored talk of his playmates, the messages of the mass media, or even the rough rhetoric of the streets. All too often the schoolroom door is opened for him by teachers who behave, says Dorothy Higginbotham later in this volume, "as though language as realized in speech were an accomplished fact at school entry." And thus begins the pervasive influence of the first major illusion about speech communication training in the elementary school: first grade Johnny can talk, so we can forget about that, and do something instead about why Johnny can't read, add or subtract, form his letters, or name the state capitals.

It is indeed true that Johnny *can* talk, sometimes too much, and sometimes when not called upon. But much of that talk, if his parents or his teachers would really take the time to listen to it, is inchoate and inconsequential, inconstant and indecorous. And it is the kind of talk, if Johnny is not exposed to some direct instruction and to some good models and to some fun in doing it, that provides the base for that inadequate adult talk that Harry Overstreet characterized in *The Mature Mind:* "In no area of our maturing . . . is arrested development more common than in the area of communication. . . . The person who is mature in his communicative powers is noted as an exception to the rule. The person who is immature—halting, clumsy, obscure, rambling, dull, platitudinous, insensitive—is the rule."

A second major illusion about speech communication training in the elementary and junior high schools is identified by a former executive secretary of the National School Boards Association: "One of the greatest fallacies in modern public education is the general belief that speech education is concerned primarily with teaching students the mechanics of pleasant voice production." Undoubtedly there are still heard in some classrooms echoes of the old school elocutionary training that generated this false notion—the how-now-brown-cow laryngeal gymnastics, or exercises in the rise and fall of the gesture. There is no doubt that at one time every schoolroom in America must have known that boy who stood upon the burning deck, and however he may have been victimized by a literary hotfoot, his very pervasiveness cast a pall over what many persons thought to be "teaching speech."

While these two grand illusions have been in the main responsible for the inadequacy of our attention to Johnny's talk in the elementary and junior high schools, there have been other contributing factors. Ruth Strickland identifies one in an essay in this volume: "Some teachers in the past treated spoken English as if it were inferior to written English rather than a different form." Wendell Johnson long ago named another in his article "You Can't Write Writing," and we must suppose that many baffled teachers would insist also that their students "can't talk talking." Still another is the seemingly common and stultifying notion that what goes on in classrooms must always be impersonal in content and, above all, in language; but by its very nature, oral discourse tends to be personal, to reflect personality. In sum, in far too many classrooms, and for a variety of reasons, the spoken word is apparently not one of the language arts. In this volume of essays we earnestly recommend a four-square language arts gospel: reading, writing, speaking, listening. And we try to be concretely helpful about how to develop a speech program.

In a way I am sorry that we could find no room in this volume for a report on "talk" in the classrooms of England, for my own views about speech education in the elementary and junior high schools certainly owe much to James Britton, Glyn Lewis, Denys Thompson, and other friendly participants from Great Britain in the Anglo-American Seminar on the Teaching of English. The essence of what we learned from our visitors was that speech (they insisted on calling it "talk," and upon ignoring their educationist countrymen who prefer "oracy") received very little isolated attention in the elementary schools, but that it tends to go on much of the time in the best schools, encouraged, unfettered and exploratory, and involving all of the class, not just two-way exchanges with the teacher. Moreover, the hope of the teacher is not to slip in oral drills or to seize opportunities to "correct" pronunciation faults, but rather to avoid anything that will make the children self-conscious. Thus he limits his function to occasional "nudging" that will encourage talking freely and creatively.

The result of all this kind of talk (the term was used as synonymous with discussion or conversation) is an alertness in dialogue situations. From this, in turn, evolves much of the students' readiness to accept the dialogue of drama, a constantly unifying element not only in the early grades but well on into classes of teenagers, moving from mime, pantomime, and improvisation to the enacting of dramas worked up in the classroom. From this kind of playmaking the English students progress to script writing (and all the while they are reading aloud the dialogues from plays in their literature study) and staged performances, simply for their own education and not for outside audiences.

Out of this total experience with rhetorical and poetic discourse, the British teachers felt that in their best schools the students were given an opportunity to learn by doing, not just by reading about doing. They felt that the doing of group talk, and the doing of drama as creators and actors, was a superior method of developing facility with language skills, strengthening creative impulses, and making students more at home in a cultural world of predominantly verbal symbols. They may be right. If all this can actually be done by the teacher's "nudging" and without explicit practice in the forms and modes of speech, so much the better. In any case, we can agree that freeing a child's feelings through creative talking and writing, encouraging his sensitivity to language and the symbolizing process, and helping him relate verbally to his world must be central in his educational experience.

American teachers especially may need also to consider how skill and pleasure in talking and listening affect the complementary skills of writing and reading. Although some studies reveal that in adult life we spend three times as many daily hours in talking-listening as we do in writing-reading, the four language arts do relate to each other. Speech teachers will particularly want to note that children who do not talk much, at home or in school, are not likely to have much to write about either. And because they will not have learned much about what makes speech communication clear, vivid, and persuasive, they are not likely to have meaningful standards by which to judge their writing. Let John Holt sum up the relationship between speaking and reading skills: "The good reader [skilled in conversation] enters into an active dialogue with the writer. He converses with him, even argues with him. The bad reader [unskilled in conversation] is passive; the words do not engage his mind; he is like a bored listener at a lecture."

The purpose of this introduction is not to say what those whose essays follow will say, but only to give the reader a kind of feeling for the points of view, rhetorical and educational, that temper today's thinking about teaching speech in the elementary and junior high schools—and perhaps to add just a touch of exhortation to do better next semester!

It is up to our contributors to provide us with fresh statements about old subjects. Dorothy C. Higginbotham does this first in formulating comprehensive proposals for the development of a total speech program. The essentially symbol-centered nature of speech is then explored by Ruth G. Strickland in writing about teaching oral language, and by John W. Black in treating the teacher's opportunities for improving the speech of children. Coming sequentially in this volume and in the elementary-junior high school speech program, the second set of three essays deals with speech skills that must be (in the American view of things) more systematically treated. Geraldine Brain Siks contributes an essay on teaching drama, Jeré Veilleux on teaching oral reading, and Carroll C. Arnold on teaching formal discourse. A final essay by

Edward B. Jenkinson and Donald A. Seybold treats an overall and unending problem for teachers, and especially for students, of oral discourse: finding something to say.

Without the contributors, this book would not of course be, and we thank them for it. But neither would it have evolved as a likely project without the initial grant from the United States Office of Education that created the English Curriculum Study Center, the support from Indiana University that has continued the center beyond the grant period, and the dedicated work of its director, Edward B. Jenkinson, not only on this volume but on an entire series dealing with the English language arts of which this is the twelfth. While he cannot shun the editor-in-chief's burdens for the series, I cheerfully do accept responsibility for the faults of this volume.

Grateful acknowledgement is given to Jan Blough, Julia Hamilton, and Lynn Sears who typed the various drafts and proofread the galleys, and to the ever-patient editorial staff of the Indiana University Press.

This volume is a portion of the project of the Indiana University English Curriculum Study Center, which was supported through the Cooperative Research Program of the Office of Education, U.S. Department of Health, Education, and Welfare. The I.U. Center received additional financial support from the Cummins Engine Foundation, which awarded Indiana University a grant that provided funds for meetings and equipment that could not be financed by the grant from the U.S. Office of Education.

J. JEFFERY AUER

On Teaching Speech in
Elementary and Junior High Schools

On the Total Elementary School Speech Program

DOROTHY C. HIGGINBOTHAM

Professor of Speech
Southern Illinois University

There is at the present time no "total" speech program in our elementary schools. An absence of uniformity in terminology and practice makes it difficult to determine the precise amount of speech instruction present in elementary education. If speech is "the expression of ideas and thoughts by means of articulate vocal sounds," as one dictionary suggests, there is unquestionably a great deal of this behavior in our schools. One study has estimated that from 650 to 1,000 oral exchanges occur between teachers and pupils during a typical day in the elementary classroom, and, if calculated, the interaction among children would greatly increase that figure. Perhaps the very pervasiveness of this peculiarly human behavior causes many teachers to believe that their main responsibility in regard to speech is not encouragement but suppression.

Obviously, random classroom talk is not the principal focus here. The term "speech program" implies a plan or definite series of goals and instructional practices designed to accomplish some kind of speech learning. Unlike reading, art, mathematics, science, or social studies, no clearly defined area of instruction in the elementary curriculum can be consistently identified as "speech." This does not mean that efforts directed at influencing oral language behavior are totally lacking in elementary education. However, there is at present great confusion regarding the values, goals, knowledge, and methods pertinent to such instruction, and it is upon these matters that our attention will center in this examination of the total speech program in the elementary schools. This essay will review the origins and present state of elementary speech instruction, consider the appropriateness of classical rhetorical theory, which has long influenced language instruction at this level, and advance the belief that a more relevant underlying body of information should begin to serve as a basis for the development and execution of elementary school speech programs.

The term "speech" implies different things to different teachers and pupils in the elementary grades. To the child who has an articulation problem, it may suggest the word and sound games he and a small number of other children play with a lady who visits their school once or twice each week. In a few schools, speech is identified with an itinerant teacher who regularly conducts speaking and listening lessons for all children in the classroom. Some of these teachers are creative dramatics specialists who work with language and creativity through the planning, playing, and evaluating of informal drama. In the junior high school, speech occasionally appears in the curriculum in a course which typically consists of student participation in such activities as public speaking, oral interpretation of literature, discussion, and parliamentary procedure. More often, oral language activities at the upper elementary level take the form of an occasional book review in English class, a rare report in social studies or science, and informal question and answer sessions conducted by teachers during the course of the day's work.

Although special teachers of speech are found in some city systems, most speech training in the elementary schools is undertaken by the regular classroom teacher under the rubric of language arts. Traditionally, the language arts curriculum has been composed of reading and writing instruction, with speaking and listening treated as incidental and receiving little attention beyond unplanned and often aimless classroom talk. When this is the practice, the mere presence of considerable oral exchange has frequently been sufficient to allay any feeling of obligation the teacher may have had for the language development of his pupils. This has been true in spite of the fact that, even in informal classroom communication, the teacher, without realizing it, often dominates the dialogue.

The majority of elementary teachers are conscientious, however. Because they are aware that the child's ability to communicate is basic to his development, they do attempt to comply with the recommendations for oral language instruction as set forth in college language arts courses, teachers' manuals, local curriculum guides, and popular periodicals specializing in instructional methodologies for the elementary schools. Unfortunately, much of this material has little relevance for the basic communication needs of children. The goals for oral language as identified in many language arts sources are lofty and vague. For example, typical broad objectives selected at random from a variety of texts included the following: to learn to appreciate beautiful spoken language, to acquire the skills necessary to use language effectively, to participate competently in one's own society, to find satisfaction in speaking, and to develop creative oral expression. The means proposed to achieve these ends usually involve experiences in oral reading, choral speaking, discussion, show-and-tell, reports, dramatics, puppetry, conducting meetings, and a variety of other situational ventures which may be only tangentially related to the general goals. This activity-centered approach tends to emphasize "effectiveness" and "correctness" in practicing oral skills identified with the mode of presentation and may reflect the teacher's own experience with the formal activities of some past high school or college speech course. Many teachers who resist this focusing on the niceties of speech performance have subscribed to the equally unproductive notion that oral language activities have their own built-in values which are so totally intangible as to be unamenable to direct instruction and the rigors of evaluation.

In spite of growing demands to the contrary, teacher-training institutions have continued to slight the oral skills in language arts courses and to treat them in a superficial way which, at its worst, leads to activity for activity's sake. As a result, too many teachers are poorly prepared to interpret and evaluate the growing body of literature and research in language and communication or to develop their own pertinent objectives and practical procedures for speaking and listening instruction. Inadequately equipped to make use of the best in new knowledge and methods, they are left little recourse except to provide children with random oral experiences in the vain hope that they are fulfilling some worthwhile, though poorly defined, need. Such an approach accomplishes good only by accident and is hardly adequate to develop the communication potential of all children.

Historical Perspective

Practices dominating much of today's speech instruction are the product of a history marred by long delay in adapting new knowledge to the classroom and by inter-disciplinary conflict. Furthermore, it is highly probable that the classically derived and traditionally executed programs of speech instruction found at the higher levels of education have adversely affected and impeded the development of a dynamic and educationally significant program of speech instruction in the elementary schools. This has occurred not through any deliberate intent or misguided effort on the part of speech people, but rather as a result of devotion to a body of theory and instructional methods which are largely inappropriate to the communication needs of young children.

From colonial times until the beginning of the present century, reading, writing, and spelling comprised almost the entire curriculum of the elementary schools. All reading was essentially oral until the twentieth century; consequently, some speech instruction was introduced into the curriculum through this medium. "Piece speaking," the recitation of memorized literary passages, was also a regular feature of many classrooms. Reflecting the elocutionary speaking style of the day, most nineteenth-century speech instruction consisted of little more than admonishing children to read and recite with attention to audibility, enunciation, articulation, and pronunciation. There was little apparent concern for communication of ideas, although one popular college speech text of the early nineteenth century suggested that "one should read as he would speak" in order to convey meaning. Not many elementary teachers were influenced by the advice, if, indeed, they were aware of it.

By the middle of the nineteenth century, the rise of humanism prompted educators to begin to write of the needs of man as an articulate being in a practical world. With the recognition that man is a speaking as well as a reading citizen, there developed some interest in broadening speech instruction in a more practical direction. Curricular methods began to be proposed which would bring question and answer periods, conversation, and discussion into more prominence in the classroom. It was even suggested that the child's own experiences as translated into everyday language be integrated into the learning process, a view widely held by contemporary educators. Unfortunately, the best of theories failed to have much impact on classroom procedures, for teachers were usually poorly educated and dissemination of information was inadequate. As a result, the interest in oral reading and reciting with narrow mechanical emphasis on voice and diction still prevailed at the close of the nineteenth century. At about this time, printed matter was becoming widely available, and with the increased circulation of newspapers, magazines, and books, silent reading began to be stressed at the upper elementary levels. This emphasis brought even less attention to oral communication.

During the first half of the twentieth century, any change or growth in speech instruction at the elementary level was exceedingly slow in spite of the introduction of more permissive educational practices and the increasing insistence by reading specialists that more attention be given to oral communication. Although speech courses have been present in American higher education since colonial days, speech as a field of study has never assumed a very direct or productive role in the education of elementary school children.

Unlike the developmental pattern of many other disciplines, speech as a separate area of study has begun in colleges and universities and moved downward through the curriculum. From the beginning, the content of upper-level speech courses in this country has been dominated by the classical notion of speech as art, and the pattern of instruction has developed around the Ciceronian concept of five procedures in preparing and performing an act of communication: invention (discovery and analysis of ideas), arrangement (organization of ideas), style (selection of appropriate language), memory (mental grasp of the material to be communicated), and delivery (presentation of material with suitable control of voice and body). The methods teachers have employed in guiding students to acquisition of these skills have traditionally involved a variety of individual platform-speaking performances ranging from reading or reciting prose, poetry, drama, and non-original speeches, to debate, oratory, and other forms of original public address. The typical instructional procedure has been assignment, performance, and criticism. In short, based on a level of acquired language proficiency presumably already attained, formal experiences in communicating are contrived as a vehicle for enhancing speaking skill to the level of artistry. At the same time, it is claimed that the skills learned in this way may be generalized to informal communication situations as well.

By 1930, this traditional or classical pattern of university speech instruction had moved into the curriculum of many secondary schools and some junior high schools. During the past thirty years, there has been evidence of an inclination to extend the pattern throughout the elementary grades. An important feature of the curricular expansion of speech which has implications for the elementary school is the amazing similarity of course content and methodology that has persisted regardless of the level of instruction. This is especially unfortunate at the elementary level, where the traditional pattern exhibits little concern for the important early stages that must precede the approach to speech as an art.

Today, speech classes are found in some elementary schools, and a few large city systems have even organized departments of speech. However, the trend toward specialization and departmentalization at this level has never become widespread for several reasons: (1) it is costly; (2) specialists in speech at this level are in short supply; and, probably most important, (3) this approach to oral language instruction is not compatible with the growing trend away from specialization and fragmentation of the elementary curriculum. Whenever speech has become a separate area of study, it has tended to emphasize differences rather than similarities in reading, writing, speaking, and listening skills. No doubt this attitude is due in part to a desire to recognize the important place of speech in the total education of the individual so that it will not be relegated, as in the past, to a position of merely supportive skill treated incidentally in the framework of some other discipline. Whatever the reason, any elementary curriculum which disregards the interrelatedness of communication skills is jeopardizing the total growth of its children.

The traditional or art emphasis in speech instruction suffers also from exclusiveness. Throughout a history spanning 2,500 years, speech as an educational discipline has had two prominent avowed purposes: training for leadership and training for excellence in the use of the spoken word. Speech as traditionally taught has always had its strongest appeal for the "good" student, the one who aspires to leadership, the gregarious and socially successful, and the student already above average in the use of language. In other words, it has been training for a favored minority of the population. The reticent student, the slow learner, the child still in the process of developing basic communication skills, the user of other than standard language patterns—for these and many others, the typical speech program has provided little that is relevant to their special communication needs.

Concepts Underlying Development of a Total Speech Program

For want of a clearer and more appropriate course to follow, teachers have gone along with the language-as-art view that has so influenced speech instruction at all levels. However, as researchers and theorists reveal an increasing body of information supporting the important role of oral communication in the intellectual as well as the social development of the child, the treatment of speech instruction as primarily an enrichment function is being revealed as inadequate. The new knowledge about child language must be brought to bear on instructional programs if the full language potential of all children is to be activated for maximum utility. Present thinking suggests at least four concepts which should influence any effort to devise a total speech program for the elementary schools. Others may evolve as the knowledge of child language continues to develop, but, for our purposes, the following will be considered:

1. The concept of speech as the basic human communication behavior from which all other language skills are derived.
2. The concept of speech as a series of complex skills acquired and developed according to a regular pattern which is subject to delay and premature termination.

3. The concept of speech communication as a factor in the development of the thinking processes.
4. The concept of speech as behavior affected by and affecting the environment and life style of the individual.

The emphasis here is on language as a developing process requiring direct as well as indirect instruction. In addition, a total speech program in the elementary schools should recognize the important function of speech in the acquisition of the secondary skills of reading and writing, in the process of thinking and learning, and in the personal and social adjustment of the individual to his environment.

Interrelatedness of Communication Skills

Communication has become a popular word in education—one that is being used with increasing frequency to represent a functional approach to the skills long identified as language arts. Learning to listen, speak, read, and write continues through life, but research suggests that the first twelve to fifteen years are the optimum time for acquiring proficiency in these skills. It is during this period that our schools have the greatest responsibility and opportunity for guiding the individual child toward realization of his full communication potential. The early development of all verbal skills is basic to later school work and success in life.

Language as communication is the concept that inextricably links all of the language-related skills. These skills— listening, speaking, reading, and writing—are acquired through the need to communicate, and it is only through their continued use that they grow and develop. Language is a complex system of symbols, and, although it is not easy to learn to manipulate the system in all of its forms, the learning process is greatly facilitated by the teacher who understands and utilizes the relationships among the various language skills.

The child, as a listener, is first a receiver of communication. The infant hears language symbols before he is able to attach meaning to them, but he may respond with a look, smile, or cry when a familiar voice is manipulated in a particular way. At first, the response occurs independently of the verbal content of the message. The prelinguistic period, however, is relatively short; through listening and observing, the child soon begins to be aware that certain sounds are related to people, objects, or acts. This awareness is followed by his own efforts at naming, that is, the initial attempts to attach verbal symbols to the environment. By the age of three or four, children have developed a high degree of skill in using language symbols to represent and affect their environment. The child has progressed from only receiving and decoding messages to encoding and transmitting them in the symbols he has acquired. He has learned most of the sounds, basic structural patterns, and a great many of the words of the language; he has developed accompanying intonation, rate, and even gestures. Learning to communicate orally is a major preoccupation in the early years of childhood. It is a process involving complex and not yet well-defined innate factors, and it is highly correlated with the quantity and quality of interaction with speech models available for imitation and stimulation.

No act of communication is complete without the sending and receiving functions demonstrated here by speaking and listening. In communicating through speech, the *basic* form of any living language, the sender encodes his thoughts and feelings into symbols that he transmits orally; the receiver hears and decodes the oral symbols. The encoding process is dependent upon the speaker's having in his reserve of experience the language symbols and structures with which to represent his thoughts. The decoding process requires that the listener's language be sufficiently approximate to the speaker's so that some degree of meaning can be attached to the message received. Both the encoding and decoding processes demand that sender and receiver have internalized the language's structural and phonological systems as well as its meaning.

The secondary communication skills of reading and writing are extensions of the primary skill of speaking. The thought processes involved in these secondary skills are dependent upon what is already stored in the mind through speaking. The graphic code in reading and writing is simply another set of symbols that represents the oral symbols of speech; written symbols are representations of the spoken language, not of the object or act for which they stand. When a child reads, he matches the graphic symbol to the oral symbol that he has already internalized through speech. It is only after associating the written symbol with its oral counterpart that the normal child is able to respond to the printed page. Reading, like listening, is a process of decoding, interpreting, and reacting, and reading instruction is comprised of helping the child recognize the printed form of the language that he already uses and understands as speech. Teachers who do not recognize the relationship between the child's oral communication and his learning to read either ignore oral language development or treat it in the most aimless and erratic way. It is only by chance if these teachers provide the speech experiences needed by many children before they are able to break the written code and begin to operate as independent readers.

Skill in writing is similar to that in speaking except that the encoding process in writing involves the production of graphic symbols to represent speech symbols already internalized. It is less dynamic than speech, lacking the intonational and other features that enhance meaning in the spoken language. In addition, written language is addressed to an absent receiver who cannot provide the stimulation and feedback so vital in oral communication. It is not too surprising that many children do not respond eagerly to their initial experiences in writing.

Reading and writing cannot be treated separately from speaking and listening. The child cannot be expected to understand visual symbols for words or verbal structures he has not experienced. The strong relationship among communication skills is stressed by Doris Lee and R. V. Allen in *Learning to Read Through Experience*. They maintain that there is no way, nor any need, to separate instruction in language skills. In fact, Lee and Allen believe it is important that children developing basic language skills understand the concept of language relationships. Allen and Allen's *Language Experiences in Reading* is based on the following premises:

1. What a child thinks, he can say.
2. What he says can be written (or dictated for someone to write).
3. What has been written can be read.
4. The child can read what he has written and what others have written for him to read.

Most contemporary reading theory maintains that all of the language skills are interdependent. In the initial period of development, reading and writing are highly correlated with the quantity and quality of language acquired through speaking and listening. As the child develops reading and writing skills, speaking and listening are reinforced and enriched, and vice versa. Thus, any total speech program in the elementary schools must include work which will serve both a readiness and a developmental function in the acquisition of the secondary language skills.

Speech as Developmental Process

Regardless of cultural group or language, the developmental process in language learning for all children appears to follow a regular pattern, progressing from random sounds to a vastly complex syntactical network. The prelanguage stage serves a readiness function as the child cries and babbles. The first words appear at about nine to twelve months, and the basic patterns of adult grammar are present by three and a half years. Development will continue until age ten and possibly beyond, but any growth after that period appears to be built upon whatever skills have preceded it.

If the pattern of language acquisition is the same for all children, what does account for the great variation in language performance among individuals? The answer may be found not in the pattern of development but in rate and extent of acquisition, which vary according to native endowment and environmental stimulation.

Language cannot develop in a linguistic vacuum. Its acquisition is, to a great extent, dependent upon interaction with others, and the intensity and quality of that relationship affects the language development. Parents and other family members are the first and most important language tutors. The largely indirect methods employed by these early teachers vary, depending primarily upon the nature of family life and parental attitudes and methods in relating to children. To develop his language capacity, the child must have the benefit of constant feedback, best obtained from a running dialogue with an adult. The mother, as the most constant adult figure in the child's early environment, is probably his most influential teacher. The quality of the dialogue she carries on with her child can be measured in terms of its success as a model and motivator for the maturing language behaviors requisite to his intellectual, emotional, and social growth. If it is to be beneficial, the dialogue of the adult must be rich in meanings for the child, allowing him to expand his language, verbalize experiences, and seek and use questions and answers. The child ought to hear and experiment with a variety of syntactic structures and grammatical forms. In short, the adult language model should provide the example and experience the child needs if he is to progress from the simple to the complex and from the concrete to the abstract in language and thought. Without much conscious awareness, fairly well educated families supply the kinds of language stimulation the child requires for normal progression in the development of language. Unfortunately, there are also many environments which fail to provide adequate adult-child interaction with the result that by school age the child is typically far below expected norms in all aspects of language performance.

Psychologists stress the first four years as the most crucial for language learning, emphasizing that deprivation can have far greater consequences during this early period than at a later age. An important finding which researchers have observed in studies of child language is what they have labeled the "cumulative deficit phenomenon." The child who is low in early language achievement does not catch up or even hold his own in language and learning skills even after exposure to the traditional school environment. In fact, the child's deficiency becomes more marked as he continues through school.

Without special attention to the urgent language deficiencies of the linguistically disadvantaged child, the gap between his school achievement and the national median grows wider with each passing year. The findings of research on language acquisition, relationship between language performance and school success, and optimal learning times lead to the conclusion that the critical periods for coping with problems of language development are the preschool and early school years. Thus, the amount of *relative* success teachers can expect from their efforts to add to or change basic language behaviors after the elementary years is negligible.

Speech and the Thought Processes

Although speech has long been valued as the principal tool for social adaptation, only in the past twenty years has there been much systematic effort to discover its relationship to thought. Many psychologists have now come to believe that language in the form of internalized speech is a central component of the thinking processes, with particular relevance for cognitive development.

It hardly needs to be demonstrated that language plays a role in thought, but the precise nature and extent of the relationship is not yet fully understood. To claim that language and thought are the same or that one is totally dependent upon the other is to pursue theories belabored by experts and found wanting. Lev Vygotsky, eminent

Russian psychologist, maintained that external speech (interpersonal communication) turns thoughts into words. Inner speech (intrapersonal communication), on the other hand, turns speech into inward thought and becomes the internal dialogue which Vygotsky believed necessary for generalizing, categorizing, inferring, and problem solving. Many Russian and Western psychologists agree with Vygotsky's notion that language not only shapes but may even lead the earlier development of cognitive processes. However, it is widely accepted that much thinking occurs without language; one school of psychological thought contends that language merely reflects rather than determines cognitive development. Of course there is still much to be settled in the relationship between language, speech, and cognition, but it seems clear that, while language may not be the only instrument of cognition, it plays an important role in varying forms of cognitive functioning.

Acquiring language is in itself an intellectual process of progressive complexity. At the outset, the child probably acquires his first small vocabulary through a kind of conditioning provided by people around him. If the child hears "mama" often enough and is rewarded for saying the word, he will begin to use it in relation to that woman who satisfies many of his needs. Instead of serving as the symbol for the object, however, the first words are more likely the child's simple assigning of another attribute, a name, to the person, act, or object being identified. The process of learning language becomes much more highly intellectualized when the child realizes that everything has a name, a concept he may not have until about the age of two. It is with this understanding that he goes out to meet the language, so to speak, and in his newly developing awareness actively begins to seek the labels for things.

Vygotsky states that it is at this time that the knot is tied in the relationship between thought and language. From this point forward, the connection grows stronger as thinking and speaking evolve, and the two processes become highly interdependent. It should be noted, however, that neither psychologists nor linguists have yet been able to establish a correspondence between the early phases of language acquisition and the level of cognition. There is a growing body of evidence which indicates that, at least in the early stages, language is acquired through a separate system rather than as a part of general cognitive development.

Through social communication the child learns much more than isolated concepts represented by single words. The initial period of single word usage is soon followed by the combining and arranging of words according to the language's grammatical rules of formation and transformation. The use of structure seems somewhat crude at first with the omission of many words (articles, prepositions), but content words, rich in meaning, are used in the accepted order ("disa kitty" not "kitty disa") so that the message is clear. Structures become progressively more complete in the child's language performance; by the age of three many children are using most of the basic structural patterns commonly found in adult speech. It is likely that the language patterns acquired in normal development play an important role in reshaping and expanding meaning for storage in the child's bank of experiences. The extent to which he can make future use of past experiences is thought to be greatly facilitated by this ability to translate into language the intricacies and implications of experience.

Psychologist Jerome Bruner believes that, as the child is learning to control language as an instrument of thought, he progresses through three techniques for representing reality: action, imagery, and symbols. These three levels comprise a hierarchy of increasing complexity in cognitive functioning. The enactive mode, the earliest stage, is a "here-and-now" kind of development which entails representing things and activities in actions. During this period, the first year or two of development, the child acts out, labels, points to, and comments about what he is immediately experiencing in his environment. The second level of development involves a higher form of behavior—using language to reflect upon what has been stored from previous experience. The child then can think about experiences he has had and talk about them, using structures which allow him to express a more remote view of his world. However, he is still in a concrete stage in the sense that he must have stored experience in the absence of the real thing. Bruner terms this the ikonic or imaging stage; he believes it reaches its high point between the ages of five and seven. During this period the child is benefited by many concrete experiences requiring him to answer questions and solve problems in connection with an action situation. It is important that along with the content experience he be given the language structures that identify discovered relationships. For example, the child may have learned the structure words "if " and "because" as a result of dialogue with an adult *before* he is able to use them successfully in solving a problem in his own everyday experience. When children become deliberately conscious of a mental process through their further experience of symbolizing that process in speech, they have made a step necessary to generalizing experience to other situations and thereby are able to move upward in the hierarchy of conceptual thinking. In other words, the mediation which language provides enables the child to develop the abstract thought required for different levels of generality. The most difficult words, but ones extremely important for storing operations, are the abstract structure words such as "if," "although," "to," "from," "because," "in," "out of," and "for." Through direct and indirect means, children can be guided in converting their experiences into these and other definitive symbols for storage so that internal reflection and review will be possible.

The third stage, the symbolic level in Bruner's hierarchy, occurs near the age of adolescence. This is a time when highly abstract thinking appears, and the child begins to see beyond concrete relationships to possible or hypothetical ones. Of this period, Bruner says: "It is evidenced by an ability to consider propositions rather than objects; concepts become more exclusively hierarchical in structure; alternative possibilities can be handled in a combinatorial fashion." Once children have gained the ability to translate experience into language or some other symbolic form, they are able to acquire new knowledge without immediate experience. The child's ability to operate at this level of thought seems very much related to the linguistic development that has gone before. This again raises the question whether attention to language may have a direct bearing upon acquisition of cognitive skills. Although some argue that special linguistic intervention has little effect on cognitive development, Bruner and his associates believe that training a child to use language appropriately related to a task will aid him in performing the required operation. If language is not the sole instrument of thought, its use in this type of communication is closely tied to cognitive development.

While the exact nature of the role of language and communication in cognitive functioning is not fully understood, it seems clear that school experience as well as preschool home training in language and cognition are important to cognitive growth. Some children may acquire the desired language proficiency through dialogue at home and in school; many, if not most, do not. Recognition of the place of language in cognition and cognitive development and understanding of the hierarchical nature of intellectual growth should be reflected in the pattern of preschool and elementary school speech instruction. Surely here, more than in any other area of child development, lies the greatest promise and challenge to elementary education.

Speech and the Environment

Although a common pattern of development seems to occur in acquiring the basic characteristics of any native language, there are differences among societal groups in the values placed upon language as a means of communication and in the styles and uses of language. In *Studies in Cognitive Growth,* Bruner discusses the role of language in different cultures. He reasons that, in our own technical society, life has become increasingly complex, and learning situations are often removed from their original action context. For example, a child may see a bottle of milk deposited on the doorstep each day yet have little conception of the source of that product. This kind of experience, occurring repeatedly in the child's world, increases the demands on language as a means of representing the knowledge, skills, and values continually being conveyed to him. More primitive cultures, on the other hand, make greater use of concrete methods, such as showing, to impart important information and behaviors to children. Obviously, the child growing up in a society that demonstrates essentially restricted and concrete uses of language will, in many ways, be different and perhaps limited in his language mastery, for the complexity of learned language tends to be highly correlated with the demands of the early linguistic environment. This does not mean that one language is superior to another in what it *can* express, but rather that the cultural environment regulates what the language must and regularly does express with relative ease.

Within any cultural group there are individuals and subgroups who, because of the special demands of their immediate personal environment, deviate in some respects from the verbal behaviors displayed by the larger group. In the use of the common language that loosely binds our own culture, there are noticeable individual and group differences related to ethnic group, socio-economic class, geographic region, schooling, or a combination of these and other variables operating to affect the group. The deviation may be in pronunciation, vocabulary, structure, or in overall language facility in relation to some expected level of proficiency. Some differences, such as regional dialect, are tolerated by a majority of the larger society; other differences lead to suffering from irrational discrimination or, even more damaging to the individual and society, to the restriction of the development of cognitive thinking.

While limitations and restrictions exist in any cultural environment, there are, unfortunately, subgroups within our society that have in common a variety of characteristics that seem to be substantially detrimental to their children's developing linguistic capacity and performance. Some twenty percent of our school population belong to one such subgroup. These are the children of families long the victims of economic and social deprivation and now labeled *disadvantaged.* They may be of Puerto Rican, Mexican, or American Indian descent; many can only be classified as rural, urban, or migrant white; and approximately half are black. These families appear to share certain attributes potentially damaging to their children's language development:

1. There is a long family history of poverty and deprivation.
2. The parents are poorly educated.
3. They command low wages and often are irregularly employed.
4. Over half of the homes have only one parent (usually the mother).
5. There is little reading material in the home, and the adults present are often poor readers or non readers.
6. Living conditions are crowded, and there is a high level of noise and confusion.
7. The experiences the home affords the child tend to be restricted and lacking in variety.
8. A language other than English may be spoken in the home, and almost certainly the verbal exchange experienced most directly by the child is deficient for developing his fullest linguistic and cognitive potential.

A growing body of research supports the theory that it is ordinary communication in a variety of social contexts that is really essential in shaping language and cognitive thought and that the nature of that exchange varies among socio-economic classes. In the pattern of communication within the lower-class family group, two variables seem to be significant. The first is the status-oriented organization of the family, which places adults in a highly dominant position in family life and tends to exclude children from full participation in a dialogue with the parent. The communication of parent to child is often marked by a high proportion of commands (Shut up!, Stop that!, Do this!) offering few alternatives in either action or language; very little communication involves the child in language used for explanation, reflection, planning, or problem solving.

A second factor that may be operating to restrict the language development of children from the lower socioeconomic groups is the lack of cross-cultural communication. This observation is at least in part based on Vygotsky's theory that the closer the psychological contact between people and the more understandings they share, the less speech is needed for them to communicate. Interaction requiring little verbal communication occurs between close friends, husband and wife, mother and child, and, in general, between those living in constant close association. Children who seldom have contact outside their immediate environment may never develop beyond "family talk."

These environmental limitations are thought to be constituent elements in the development of what sociologist Basil Bernstein calls the "restricted code," a style of communication limited in vocabulary, having simple and often incomplete sentences, making little use of subordination for elaboration, being highly implicit rather than explicit in meaning, and lacking in specificity. It is a kind of verbal shorthand that carries a maximum of general meaning with a minimum of language. The restricted code is not limited to the lower class, for within the middle-class family group the child at various times and stages also makes use of this communication style. But, as a result of the demands of communication in a *variety* of situations, the middle-class child usually develops an elaborated style as well. Many of those who comprise the lower socio-economic class, however, live in a caste or closed society affording little opportunity for communication beyond the immediate, intimate group. The result is a highly restricted style of speech that is often the *only* language experienced by these children during the critical years when linguistic and cognitive skills are most easily acquired. While it has not yet been positively established that social-class differences in language are the cause of cognitive differences, a promising body of evidence is beginning to accumulate in support of the theory.

Children limited in experiencing the requirements imposed by communication may have difficulty differentiating between speech for self and speech for others, expressing themselves in a comprehensible way, mastering a wide range of structural options and sentence types, producing and securing answers to a variety of forms of questioning, recognizing and expressing relationships in verbal problem solving, finding word options to represent their thoughts and feelings, recognizing and interpreting paralinguistic cues (pitch, volume, rate, intonation, gestures) to the feelings of others, and adjusting to the comprehension of the receivers of their communication. Any child, regardless of social class, will be handicapped in his cognitive as well as his social development if his opportunities to participate in these and many other behaviors practiced in ordinary communication are substantially impeded. Socially, communication with others is necessary if the child is successfully to develop his self-concept and broaden his view to take into account the perspective of others; however, it is the amelioration of environmentally induced restricted communication experience, with its consequent effect upon thinking and learning, that is the most pressing educational need of many children.

Unfortunately, many teachers are far more disturbed by nonstandard usage than by the child's deficiencies in communicating. Part of this may be due to a middle-class snobbishness which rejects as inferior and unacceptable any gross deviations from standard dialect. The "prestige" speech of this nation is the English language dialect most widely used in the educational system, in the courts, in religion, and in commerce. No more correct than any other dialect, it is, however, identified by teachers as "good usage" or "correct grammar." Too often speech that is merely different is thought to be deficient or abnormal. At this time, there is no proof that any language or dialect is inherently inferior as an instrument of thought or social communication; nevertheless, speakers of nonstandard English are often penalized both socially and economically by the larger society. In school, the speaker of a nonstandard dialect may be subjected to great pressures from his teacher to speak the language in ways quite different from what he is accustomed to hearing at home or among friends and people he respects and admires. If his nonstandard speech continues into adulthood, he may experience considerable social and job discrimination if he attempts to move into the larger societal group.

The problems surrounding the teaching of standard English are political and moral as well as educational. If members of a minority group are to be integrated as full and complete members of the larger society, it seems appropriate to add to any nonstandard dialect one which will ensure that the individual will not be discriminated against on the basis of his language. (Of course, if it is realistic to assume that a minority group will remain separate from the majority and that its individuals will have no occasion to communicate outside the immediate society, then it may also be argued that there is no need to be concerned about acquiring a second dialect.) The ability to speak more than one dialect may be beneficial to many members of an integrated society, and surely teachers need far more knowledge and skill concerning dialects than they now have. Teachers have a responsibility to respect the child as a whole individual, including whatever dialect he brings with him from his home. This moral obligation should take precedence over every other consideration in teaching communication.

Language instruction in the elementary schools has tended in the past to ignore the compelling needs of different societal groups. As a consequence, many children have been unnecessarily handicapped in learning as well as in social adaptation. An educational system devoted to equality of opportunity must recognize that linguistically, intellectually, and socially what the child is and what he will become are closely related to both his home and school communication experiences. Thus, any relevant speech program at the elementary level must focus primarily upon environmentally derived deficiencies in the ability to communicate.

The Need for Instruction in the Affective Domain

Throughout, our discussion has centered on the cognitive domain in an attempt to emphasize the important, though much neglected, relationships between cognition and communication in the process of acquiring knowledge and developing intellectual skills. At the same time, however, we could not support any curricular program which ignored the basic role of the affective domain in the total development of the child. Of great importance, though difficult to define in behavioral terms, affective behaviors are those related to the feelings and emotions of the individual. It is in this realm of development that attitudes, values, adjustment, and motivation are classified. The child's adjustment and achievement in school are greatly dependent upon how he feels about himself and others and upon how he perceives events in his environment.

There should be no conflict in educating both the emotions and the intellect. Meaningful education cannot separate the two. Although the precise nature of the relationship between intellect and the affective domain is not clearly understood, a strong tie exists. It would be a mistake to become so preoccupied with overt behavioral manifestations of language and cognition that we ignored the child's more covert emotional states, which bear so powerfully upon his ability to think and communicate.

Speech may not be the answer to all of the child's communication needs. In efforts to heighten emotional sensitivity, nonverbal experiences are often most effective; feelings are not always easily expressed in words. Terry Borton, an educator and author committed to affective education, recently wrote: "Education that deals with feelings is often facilitated by skipping over the verbal labels which have been learned relatively late in life, regaining the other senses, and then reintegrating them with verbal thought and new behaviors." This suggests that the enactive mode of representation may be an important instructional device throughout the elementary school years. In addition to recognizing and expressing his own self-awareness, the child must learn to understand and cope with communication barriers between himself and others if he is to participate meaningfully in the dialogue which is so basic in his intellectual and emotional growth. If the means to that end are largely nonverbal, they should be no less a matter of concern to the teacher intent upon "speech" instruction. It is becoming increasingly apparent that *communication* and not language or speech should be the focus of our instruction.

"Experience" and "involvement" are expressions used with great frequency by educators intent upon making the child an active instead of a passive participant in the learning environment. Such an instructional attitude has great potential for the child's growth, both in knowledge and in sensitivity. The classroom experience should not be a launching platform for cognitive development without regard for its potential as a generator of heightened emotional awareness. Involvement can be unrealistic and experiences nonproductive when the goal is the acquisition of facts or skills without regard for the emotional content possibly imbedded in the situation. Sensory and intellectual awareness of one's own feelings is necessary if one is to learn to empathize with others in the immediate environment as well as with peoples and events of the past.

A serious obstruction to any learning situation is the excessive aggression or, at the other extreme, severe reticence of some children. Nonverbal as well as verbal communication experiences can help the child develop emotional behaviors that are productive rather than destructive to the self and others. Through interaction, children can be led to the awareness and control of their emotional states and can experience the joy of satisfying relationships with others. Instruction aimed at improving communication skills must be directed to both the cognitive and affective domains, and development in either area should not be left to chance.

The Need for a New Curriculum

Up to this point we have mentioned weaknesses in the present elementary program as it relates to verbal communication. We have proposed that a new body of information available through recent and continuing research be brought to bear on education. If we accept an expanded view of speech instruction, we must be prepared to adjust our instructional goals and practices to accommodate the broader perspective. A rational and constructive approach to the language behaviors of all children will provide for amelioration and development as well as enrichment so that each child may advance as far and as rapidly as possible toward his full linguistic capacity. At every level, from preschool through junior high, teachers can expect to find variations in language performance ranging from children severely delayed in development to those whose facility in communicating far exceeds that of their peers. Evaluating the child's communication behavior, setting objectives, and developing productive methods for individual children are, ultimately, responsibilities of the classroom teacher. It it is here that the success or failure of any elementary speech program must be determined.

Research suggests that after the early teens the acquisition of new language behaviors is extremely difficult. If verbal communication is as important to cognitive development and to social adaptation as is now generally supposed, it follows that the elementary school years are the critical time for developing language abilities through the medium of speech communication. Unfortunately, most elementary teachers are poorly prepared to guide the child's development of language for cognitive thinking, for communicating successfully with others, or for enrichment. The best efforts of teacher-training institutions, curriculum builders, school administrators, researchers, and speech and language specialists must be applied to the problem if teachers are to acquire the knowledge, skills, and practical means essential for improving the verbal abilities of all children.

Teacher–training institutions must devote a larger proportion of their instruction to this aspect of child education. A language arts curriculum that only briefly touches on the oral mode is not adequate to prepare the teacher to fulfill his obligation to the language needs of children. A substantial part of the elementary teacher's training should be composed of courses instructing him in (l) the acquisition of primary (listening and speaking) and secondary (reading and writing) communication skills; (2) relationships between verbal communication and thought processes with emphasis on hierarchical patterns of development; (3) language as it relates to learning in all areas of the curriculum; (4) recognition and understanding of conditions operating to produce individual differences in linguistic competence and performance; (5) development of specific objectives for instructional speech communication; and (6) selection and implementation of ameliorative, developmental, and enrichment communication experiences. Without this background in psychology of language, linguistics, and communication, teachers can only continue their aimless and unproductive treatment of this most important aspect of the elementary curriculum.

The classroom teacher cannot accomplish the task of successfully implementing a communication-oriented curriculum without the support of an understanding and innovative administration. Classrooms that encourage children to verbalize are not so quiet as those where silence is regarded as evidence that learning is taking place. Nor is rigid scheduling the ideal when teachers seek to take advantage of the spontaneous learning situations that occur frequently in any dynamic classroom environment. One promising approach to early elementary communication instruction would allow children to speak often and in their own way in an environment providing much opportunity for dialogue with an adult. Children at all levels benefit greatly from association with an adult who will talk *with* them, listen to them, answer their questions, help them experience that which is of high interest to them, and encourage them to relive their experiences verbally. Because this approach requires one-to-one communication rarely possible when the adult-to-child ratio is one to thirty, the assistance of teacher aides or paraprofessionals can be invaluable. A high degree of professional training need not be required of the housewives, college dropouts, or even high school students who assist the teacher. What is wanted is adults who like and respect children and who are willing and able to participate in a continuing dialogue with a small group of youngsters. For most schools this approach would require a considerable alteration in philosophy and staffing, but it is an innovation worthy of consideration.

Much additional research is needed if teachers are to play a more meaningful role in child language learning. The pattern of language development, including all of its constituent elements, should be more clearly identified; uncomplicated evaluation techniques must be devised to enable the teacher to assess with some certainty each child's level of development. Of equal importance is the need to identify the hierarchical stages of cognitive development and their possible relationship to various linguistic operations. If research findings are to be utilized in curricular practices, more effort should be devoted to translating and implementing new knowledge. With the growth of available information and the continual need to adapt methods, rapid and effective means must be found to communicate instructional possibilities to teachers. Researchers need to become much more involved in the dissemination of their findings; elementary teachers, on the other hand, could benefit from some training in reading research reports. Many innovative language programs applying both direct and indirect instruction to a variety of conditions are now under consideration and investigation, and the future will bring even more experimentation by classroom teachers as well as by research specialists. Some effective means must be devised to convey the most promising of these methods to the classroom teacher.

All of this implies new demands on an already overburdened and harassed elementary teacher. The task of retraining those in the field would, undoubtedly, be enormous and never entirely successful. However, workshops, in-service training programs, summer institutes, and additional schooling in updated and innovative programs, such as those financed by the Education Professions Development Act, can all be of great benefit to experienced teachers. The most far-reaching and permanent impact on child communication instruction can be made by teacher-training institutions, but changes there are slow in coming and, even when made, are not immediately felt in the field.

Until the training of all teachers can be improved, a new type of communication specialist could serve an important interim function in the schools. This person should not be a specialist in the narrow sense of the speech correctionist, creative dramatics teacher, or reading consultant; rather, he should be trained in all areas vital to relevant speech and language instruction. He would serve in an advisory and supportive capacity to the classroom teacher, aiding him in setting objectives and developing appropriate communication experiences to fit the needs of each child. The long-range goal, of course, should be the reduction of the role of the specialist as all teachers are better trained.

In this era of curricular reevaluation and revision, no aspect of the elementary curriculum has a greater need for improvement or holds more promise than the area of speech communication. For a behavior so pervasive and basic as speech to continue to be treated incidentally is folly at best. A new curriculum emphasizing communication cannot be fully implemented immediately, but a beginning must be made at once if children of the next decade are to benefit.

REFERENCES

Allen, Roach Van, and Claryce Allen. *Language Experiences in Reading.* Chicago: Encyclopaedia Britannica Press, 1966.

Bernstein, Basil. "Social Structure, Language, and Learning," *Educational Research* Vol. 3, 1961, 163–176.

Borton, Terry. "Reach, Touch, and Teach." *Saturday Review,* January 18, 1969, 56–70.

Bruner, Jerome S. *Toward a Theory of Instruction.* Cambridge: Harvard University Press, 1966.

Bruner, Jerome S., Rose R. Olver, Patricia M. Greenfield, et al. *Studies in Cognitive Growth.* New York: John Wiley, 1967.

Chomsky, Carol. *The Acquisition of Syntax in Children from 5 to 10.* Cambridge: M.I.T. Press, 1969.

Lee, Dorris, and Roach Van Allen. *Learning to Read Through Experience.* New York: Appleton-Century-Crofts, 1963.

Vygotsky, Lev Semenovich. *Thought and Language.* Cambridge: M.I.T. Press, 1962.

On Teaching Oral Language in the Elementary School

RUTH G. STRICKLAND

Research Professor Emeritus of Education
Indiana University

A major miracle of the child's preschool years is his learning of his native tongue. During the years from two to five, he masters a language with a skill and concentration rarely found in older learners. Scholars are only now becoming aware of how vast, varied, and complex is the mental effort the child makes during these early years. A Russian scholar and student of children's language has called the child from two to five "the hardest mental toiler on our planet."

Though the child comes into the world with the essential physical apparatus for speech, all of it serves other major purposes and is only later put to use in speaking. The drive to learn to speak had not been considered innate by the behavioral psychologists; yet Noam Chomsky insists that the infant could not possibly learn to speak by depending solely on a trial-and-error process of imitation and repetition even if his effort is reinforced by the approval of parents and other children. Chomsky bases his conviction on the fact that the child very soon acquires the ability to produce a wide variety of sentences he has never before heard. Other primates, he reminds us, have the same physical apparatus as the child—lips, a tongue, a movable lower jaw, a larynx with vocal cords, and lungs —yet even with intensive and extended teaching, they are unable to develop speech. The entire process of learning to speak, then, may be a fitting of what is new into an innate propensity, a genetic potential with which the child is born.[1] Be that as it may, if the people who frequent the child's little universe talk to him and talk among themselves in his presence, he seems very early to take an interest in speech and to respond to it.

Children vary in their learning of speech. Some start early and learn rapidly, some later and more slowly. All normal children, however, seem to follow the same basic sequence of learning. Recent studies indicate that some children, even by their first birthday, show awareness of the melodic structure of the language. They use in their babbling the pitch, stress, and pauses characteristic of English sentences. Some strings of babbled sound follow clearly the patterns of questions, statements, and exclamations. The first words in a child's vocabulary are the meaning-bearing words in adult sentences—words pitched a little higher and emphasized a little more vigorously than the structure words. A little later there is clear evidence that the child becomes intuitively aware of the rules that govern the structure of his language. He talks about "boys," "books," and "wishes" and also about "foots," "deers," and "mouses," not only applying but overapplying his scheme for forming plurals. He does the same with the past tense of verbs, producing not only "walked," "played," "wanted," and "sang" but also "runned," "goed," "tooked," and "brang." Children learn much by imitation, to be sure, but they also sense quite early both the sound structure and the grammatical structure of their language. As they acquire vocabulary, they string words together following the patterns they hear used by others.

Every child learns to speak the language of his environment—that is all that he *can* learn. Since there are in the United States many dialects and since ours is an increasingly mobile population, the speech in any elementary school classroom may represent wide variations in phonological and intonational patterns, vocabulary, usage, and grammar. Whatever it is that the child brings with him to school, his speech—his idiolect—forms the starting point for any formal program in oral language.

Freeing the Child to Talk

The first efforts of the teacher in the primary school, and in the middle grades as well, must be planned to help each child feel comfortable, relaxed, and at home in his school environment. An informal and flexible classroom arrangement in addition to organization is essential to language growth. An English scholar at the Dartmouth conference (Anglo-American Seminar on the Teaching of English, held at Dartmouth College, summer of 1966) said, "above all we need an easy though *not* easy-going civilized atmosphere in the classroom." Children as well as most adults talk better in informal, face-to-face situations than in formal, impersonal ones. There is nothing inspirational about talking to the backs of heads and nothing more terrifying to many children than to be required to stand before a mass of faces dotted at even intervals throughout a large room. Even children who speak freely and well in out-of-school situations find adjustment difficult in the formal atmosphere of some classrooms.

A great deal of experience with language is necessary to develop it to the point where it is a ready and effective tool for all kinds of use. Although less frequently now than formerly, schools strive to keep children silent for the greater part of the school day and then drill for language improvement in a single "language period." However, the teacher works with language from the time the first child enters the room in the morning until the last one goes home at the end of the day. The entire curriculum depends on language as a means of operation, an avenue of enrichment, learning, and expression as well as an essential part of individual and group living. Yet recent surveys of the language programs in many classrooms reveal that it is the teachers, not the children, who have the lion's share of opportunity and practice. In his report of the discussion of English and American scholars at the Dartmouth conference, Herbert Muller says:

> And the neglect of talking by the schools has become stranger in the modern world where people are listening to more talk than ever before in history, on radio and television, and many are doing more talking, too, in the endless committees and conferences alike in business, government, and the professional world. In the democracies which make so much of free speech, the torrent of platitudinous, illogical, often irresponsible talk, and its acceptance by lazy, uncritical listeners, are provoking books of alarm.[2]

The Goal of Easy Use of Language

The first requisite to easy, useful speech is an atmosphere in which language can flourish. Talking must be legal—the atmosphere must be one which not only permits talk but actively stimulates and encourages it.

The second requisite is a happy, wholesome relationship between teacher and children and among the children themselves. The nature of human relationships is closely related to the quality of communication. Whether the flow of communication brings about good relationships or wholesome human relationships bring about good communication does not matter. The important point is that one is essential to the other. Many a child is isolated because a speech defect, a foreign background, or a dialect unfamiliar to the other children has caused him to be rejected. Or a child may be unable to fit into a group as a cooperative, participating member because he is over-aggressive in his use of language and thus inept in making contacts with other children. Teachers need to analyze their own use of language as well as that of the children to know whether their language encourages and supports children's expression or unwittingly suppresses it.

The third requisite for easy use of language is the presence of many dynamic, ongoing interests. There must be experiences and ideas that to the children are worth talking about if there is to be interchange. Both firsthand experience and the vicarious experience of books and other media must keep the child's vocabulary of words and meanings continuously expanding. Traditional schools often forced the child onto a language-learning plateau and cut him off from all opportunity to extend his language power while he learned to read, write, and spell the commonly known words. They turned off the fountain at its source. A program rich in literature, social studies, and science is necessary to expand the child's experience with language and lay the foundation for further development.

The Goal of Clear, Intelligible Language

Otto Jesperson, the noted Danish philologist, lists three stages or levels of language: intelligible language is the minimum level; correct language is the next and more exacting level; and finally, good language, both clear and beautiful, is at the top of the scale.[3]

Intelligible language is the first need of the elementary school program. The child must be able to express himself with ease and with the confidence that he will be understood. "Correctness" is the subject of pages of writing and volumes of talk among scholars and educators in both America and England. On one point, however, the representatives at the Dartmouth conference seemed to agree: the teacher must accept willingly and sincerely the speech the child brings to school and help him use it to enter comfortably into the life of the classroom. The English would then introduce criticism and correction "very delicately," subordinating it to the child's right to expect from his audience response to what he has said rather than to his manner of saying it. The Americans, on the other hand, tended to favor a more direct and systematic program of correction. While the English favored "nudging children along, guiding them, obliquely directing them but taking care not to 'intervene' in their natural, rightful development," the Americans were more inclined toward direct teaching of Standard English.

Intelligible speech is clear speech. Clarity of speech and language has a number of aspects: articulation of sounds, enunciation, pronunciation, usage, syntax, choice of words, and matters of voice quality and projection.

Articulation of sounds still presents a problem for some children in the primary school. The majority learn the sound patterns of the language by the age of four or five, but there are a few in almost any beginning group who substitute sounds or manipulate their vocal apparatus in such a way that the sound produced for a letter differs from the accepted one. Here the teacher must exercise great care in determining what to correct. Certainly he must help the child who says "The witto dirl tame to cool" instead of "The little girl came to school" because the sounds the child uses will cause trouble in learning to read and spell. But the standard toward which the teacher must work is the speech of educated people of the region. It would be unfortunate indeed if a teacher from Chicago attempted to make the speech of Boston or Atlanta children fit his own pattern.

Deficiencies or inaccuracies in hearing are responsible for sound substitution and poor articulation in some children. If a child learning to talk does not perceive accurately the sounds made by adults, he forms the sounds as he hears them. Unless he is given help, he continues to practice the sounds as he first learned them until, by the time he enters school, he finds it difficult to make corrections in the articulation of them. In most cases, there is no organic defect but only one of auditory perception.

Enunciation is a matter of clear-cut production of beginning and ending sounds and of giving each syllable its full value. Elision and slurring of adult speech is responsible for many of the children's confusions. Children often ask for help with spelling "how'zit," "gonna," and "neck'-n'ears." The teacher's own example of clearly enunciated speech is perhaps the most potent force for improvement. Children can be encouraged to carry on many types of activity that demand clear enunciation. The words of a song must be enunciated clearly or they are lost. The dramatization of a story falls flat if the audience cannot understand what the characters are saying. Making oral reports and sharing experiences give children an opportunity to note audience response to their efforts. Dramatization of radio and television broadcasts (or participation in real ones) motivates effort to enunciate clearly. Choral reading can afford both motivation and practice.

Pronunciation is learned from the family at home and from others with whom the child associates. Some of the mispronunciations of middle-grade children are the result of their unaided decoding of unfamiliar words in their reading; for example, "misled" may be pronounced as one syllable instead of "mis-led" with two syllables. Again, the teacher's own example is especially important in helping children to give attention to pronunciation and to feel a sense of obligation to use the form accepted by educated speakers in the region.

Usage deviations are found in most communities. Since the child mirrors the language usage of his home and neighborhood, his usage is satisfactory to him because the people who use it are acceptable to him. He has no standards other than those of the culture of which he is a part. If he has an ear for language, he may notice usage different from that of his usual cultural milieu, but it does not sound better or more correct; he may even think it queer or amusing.

The best antidote to hearing poor language at home is hearing quantities of good language at school. Adults who move into a different dialect area tend after a time to find their own speech modified in the direction of what they constantly hear. It is difficult not to be influenced by the speech of a stutterer or a person with a foreign accent. A very important asset to a language program is a teacher who speaks well and is so respected and perhaps loved by children that they unconsciously emulate his speech. A valuable contribution to many schools is the equipment for "listening posts" made available through federal or local funds. Children can don headphones and listen to recorded stories, well-read poems, supplementary material to enrich various studies, conversations—any material purchased by the school or recorded by the teacher to meet specific needs of the children and tune their ears to the target language.

The child's ability to absorb and imitate sound patterns is both an asset and a liability in a speech improvement program. His ears are assailed by the home and community speech patterns for more hours than the school ones, and this sheer overbalance of time makes school motivation all the more difficult and important.

Scholars in linguistics as well as classroom teachers are increasingly aware that no good can come from trying to eradicate the child's home usage and substitute what is considered better. The advice of a number of them is to accept wholeheartedly the language the child uses and to help him expand his control over it and his ability to think, reason, hypothesize, and do cause-and-effect analysis in it. As he grows more mature he can be helped to see the need for *adding* language that will be good anywhere and in any kind of vocational or social situation he may wish to enter. Unless the child sees value in what has come to be called Standard English and wants to acquire it, and unless the motivation comes from within, there is little permanent gain to show for the school's efforts.

Grammar is learned inductively and intuitively as the child learns his language. He uses the rules he senses and strings words together just as the people around him do it. He recognizes what, in terms of *his personal language*, sounds right and what does not sound right. The Pennsylvania Dutch sentence, "Pa threw the cow over the fence some hay," or the Southern, "He carried his girl to the party," is amusing to children who speak a different dialect. Evidence from extensive research done over a number of years supports the conviction of some linguists that formal study of grammar has little or no effect on children's speech or on their writing. Teachers and children should give attention to vivid expressions, well-chosen words, neatly turned phrases, and also to the ineffectiveness of expression which lacks these; but they need not analyze their grammatical structure.

Children can greatly enjoy playing with sentences, exploring ways of setting forth ideas and comparing the impact of varying sentence types. They can discover ways to knit together the coordinate parts of run-on sentences through the use of subordination that eliminates surplus *and's* and makes sentences clearer and more "grown-up." Work with parts of speech, definitions, and rules is more often detrimental than helpful until children develop appreciation for well-turned sentences and learn to enjoy manipulating words to achieve them.

Choice of words is important not only for clarity but for emotional impact. Children need guidance as they learn to select words that set forth their meaning clearly and accurately. A sentence such as "My mother has all kinds of flowers in her garden" may need to be challenged for accuracy. Children's seeming thoughtlessness and cruelty to other children is often due to their lack of understanding of the emotional response words can generate. They need help in learning that words can hurt or heal, destroy friendships or build them, create problems or solve them. "Dago," "Polack," "Wop," and "Nigger" are words children pick up and use with little awareness of the emotional impact on the children toward whom these words are directed. Eleanor Estes' *The Hundred Dresses* is a book that, when read to a group of children "ganging up" against a child who is different, can carry its own message of what words can do to people.

Voice quality and *projection* are important not only because they can help their user catch and hold an audience, whether of one or many, but because they stir emotional reactions in listeners. When one person has jostled another, a sincerely apologetic "I'm sorry" elicits a very different emotional response from the same words said callously and unfeelingly. The warning, "When you say that, *smile!*" calls attention to the fact that the same words said in different tones with different burdens of implication may cause widely different responses, varying perhaps from amusement or acceptance of criticism or correction to anger or determination for revenge.

Even kindergarten children are interested in analyzing what is communicated when the teacher says to a child "Eric, come here" in a lilting voice with a smile and a relaxed, appealing attitude. They can contrast how they feel and what the words convey if the teacher's voice is cold and critical and her attitude one of even mild disapproval. These words said loudly, sternly, and roughly by an adult whose facial expression is distorted by anger and whose bodily attitude is tense and menacing cause apprehension and actual fear; yet they are the same words.

Clarity in oral language is a complex of many elements, all important in themselves and in their interrelationships. Both teacher and children can profit from occasionally pulling out a strand, looking at it separately, noting its significance in human communication and interaction, plotting humane and effective ways of improving it, and setting goals toward which they agree to work cooperatively. Sometimes this will be done inconspicuously, perhaps privately, with an individual child who needs help with articulation, choice of words, acceptable usage, or with understanding what he is doing through his use of words to another child. Some of it will be done through free and frank discussion within a group or the entire class —not through pious moralizing, not through pointing a finger of blame at anyone, but through trying to get inside the skin of another person to think as he thinks and feel as he feels.

The Goal of Suitability

Children in Japan, England, and many other countries are taught to give attention to language suitable for use with different people, on varying occasions, and for different purposes. Teachers and parents in the United States frequently ignore this need or trust that the children will learn it by example, rather than by direct guidance. Some children become aware quite early that the way one responds to another child playing in the sandbox is not the way to respond to a parent or the teacher. American children are sometimes considered rude, brazen, or obnoxious, not because the children wish to be so but because no one has ever taught them otherwise. Even within the informal, democratic interaction of home, neighborhood, and school life, children can learn that language suitable for one's peers on certain occasions is less suitable for adults to whom the child wishes to show respect. A child who wants to invite a neighbor to come over to play may call, "Hey Jim, come on over!" But the child chosen to invite the principal to visit the first grade class to see their dramatization of a story may need to issue his verbal invitation quite differently. Perhaps teacher and children together may decide that the invitation should sound more like "Mr. Brown, we are going to play the story of 'Snow White and the Seven Dwarfs' this afternoon. Can you come to see our play at two o'clock?"

Just as a business letter is more formal and less personal

than a chat with a friend, conversation and discussion may differ in like manner. All of this is a part of helping children understand that, while we may use basically the same language for varying purposes, the way in which it is used must be suitable to the occasion.

The Goal of Individuality

Many young children use language with a freshness and originality that often delights their elders. Their analogies are as original as that of the two-year-old whose opposite for "nobody" was "yesbody" and their coinages as appropriate as that of the six-year-old who said, "I guess I misunderheard you." Leo Tolstoy is said to have remarked to a group of adults, "Children know more about words than you do, for it is they who so often think up new ones." Yet most children have lost this freshness in the use of language by the age of eight, possibly because they have now mastered the language they hear about them and can use it to serve all their purposes and possibly because the pressures of home and school have caused them to feel that originality is unwelcome. At no time in the history of the language have new words been coined at a greater rate nor old words taken on new meanings to meet new needs. Yet schools are accused of molding children to a conventional pattern, and in language it appears that they do just that.

Teachers need to be encouraged to recognize any evidence of freshness and originality in children and to encourage and foster it. A well-turned phrase, a colorful or unique word, a vivid or sprightly description or analogy should be welcomed and children's attention called to it, whether in speech or writing. Each child should be encouraged to be himself, to say it in his way if his way is socially acceptable, not to copy a pattern. Originality is precious in almost any medium, and in the use of language it may mark the difference between dullness and vitality.

Listening, the Other Half of the Communication Channel

Children in the elementary school need help with listening as well as with speaking. All too often the only help they receive is the admonition to listen and to pay attention. A chart in a first grade classroom listed the following "Rules for Good Listening: 1. Sit up straight; 2. Keep your hands still; 3. Keep your feet still; 4. Look at the teacher." Many a conscientious child could be so busy doing those four things that he could not possibly listen! Since listening is not so much a physical process as a mental one, it is better served by a comfortable posture in which one can forget his body and concentrate on the activity of his mind. Young children are better helped by the suggestion that all distractions such as pencils, crayons, and books be laid aside, that they sit comfortably and listen for the points the teacher wishes to emphasize. Listening for a purpose is usually better than just general, unguided listening.

Older children profit from occasional analysis of the listening process—what it is that the mind does in listening. Obviously, one must perceive and recognize the oral symbols and put into them meaning from one's own mind. It is possible to hear an unknown language as clearly as a familiar one without attaching meaning to the sounds. Also, one must react in some way to the sound combinations. Listening requires that the sounds in a sequence be put into some sort of perspective. A speaker of

English in contrast to the other languages, helps the listener with at least a portion of this process; in English strings of words are clotted together and separated from other strings by slight pauses. Also, the speaker of English points out the most important, by pitching them a little higher and emphasizing them a little more vigorously than he does the structure words. Children do better in listening, as in everything else, if they can be helped to understand not just what to do but also why and how to do it.

Listening requires attending to sounds and registering and reacting to them at the rate at which they come. Children can be helped to realize that listening provides them only one opportunity for intake. Whereas in reading one may stop to ponder or turn back to reread for clearer comprehension, in listening one has no control over rate and no opportunity to rerun the sound track. The sound flows and is gone. Therefore, following a speaker's pace while reaching out with one's mind to catch his meaning calls for intense concentration and immediate mental reaction. If a child loses the track of what is being said, he frequently cannot tune in again; or if he does, his impressions may be greatly distorted. By calling attention to the listening process and setting goals for it, teachers can help children gain the control they need for good listening.

Talk as a Means of Learning

The young child spends all his waking hours exploring his world of things and people. His curiosity leads him in all directions. He asks questions, receives answers, and talks about the answers and about the things he does and sees. As he explores, listens, and talks, he is discovering

and relating the new to what he already knows. Through
talking about the new, he creates for it his own personal
context, something only he can do because it has to be
understood in relation to his own experience. As he talks,
he verifies that he is using words that mean the same to
other people as to him, and, thus, that his use of those
words carries meaning to others.

And then, in all too many instances, the child comes to
school and finds that talk and learning through talk is
frowned upon if not actually forbidden. J. N. Britton of the
University of London has said:

> Future generations will condemn our educational policy above all
> for this reason; that we have outlawed talk from the classroom by
> our curricula, by our teaching situation, and therefore we cannot
> know the importance of talk as a means of learning.[4]

Even young children can see that talk is a social necessity if people are to relate to each other individually and
in groups. Older children are particularly interested to
learn how much of the work of the world is being done
through talk. An assignment that makes this clear is one
that asks each child to look through several pages of any
current newspaper to note what people are doing
through talk. The President of France comes to discuss
policies and problems with the President of the United
States. Important emissaries are sent all over the world to
discuss matters of political, economic, and social importance. The Congress and other law-making bodies carry
on their work through talk, as do the courts and, nearer
home, the social, religious, civic, and governmental organizations of the community. It is not difficult for children to see that a vast amount of the most important work
of the world is being done through face-to-face talk.

There is no need for teachers to contrive practice tasks

for speech in any classroom. Every elementary school program abounds in opportunities for the child to grow and learn through talk. The English have created the term "oracy" to rank with literacy as a goal of the schools. Talking, listening, and thinking can develop together in dealing with any subject in the curriculum. Children need many opportunities to exercise their speech in conversation, discussion, and exposition. There are at least the following uses to which oral language can be put, and probably others as well:

talking	reporting
conversing	explaining or directing
discussing	evaluating
sharing	solving problems
planning	expressing creative ideas

None of these is exclusive, of course, and all are intermingled at times in any classroom situation.

Talking begins as the children come into the room in the morning and enter into group and individual enterprises. There are greetings and casual remarks to make social contact in addition to assertions, questions, comments, criticisms, or reminders about what the speaker or others are doing. It is spontaneous and unorganized, and much of it is completely random talk that can give the teacher considerable insight into the children's interests and needs if he will listen to it. The talk tends to be directed to others, sometimes without any expectation of specific response. With an occasional child there may still be monologue about what he is doing or his feelings about it. Lev Vygotsky calls this monologue an intermediate stage of speech becoming only inward thought, but the child is not quite ready to carry it on in the silence of his own mind.

Conversation calls for making direct mental and social contact with others. Real-life conversation is extemporized; it is a product of the moment, the setting, and the wills and feelings of the speakers. Jean Piaget found real verbal interaction lacking among children until about age eight, but American teachers can testify to a good deal of it at the age of five. Conversation differs from random talking in that it involves a meeting of minds, a thinking and interacting on a topic that is, at least for the time, of mutual interest. A speaker does not know from moment to moment what he is going to say because he relies not only on the meaning of the words he hears but on nonverbal cues of voice, face, and body and perhaps on what is going on in the setting as well. Speakers borrow words and phrases from each other and build on each other's sentence constructions. Real conversation is more apt to occur between two people or in a small group because it is a tossing of ideas and responses back and forth with the contributions to the conversation stemming from thought and experience. Since it calls for thinking and listening as well as speaking, it requires self-discipline, consideration, and basic good manners. The larger the group the greater the need for self-discipline and also for accepting the role of active participant, not passive onlooker.

In the elementary school, conversation takes place as children carry on activities around a worktable, at lunch time, while they take care of chores around the room, and as they prepare for or clean up after various sorts of activities. With younger children, it is often stimulated by contributions to the show-and-tell period and, with older children, by opportunities to share their outside-of-school interests and their reading. The teacher may guide the conversation through comments, questions, or suggestions to give it depth, to keep it from degenerating into argument or idle chatter, and to help children develop skill and independence.

All that is said of conversation is true of discussion, with at times the added compulsion of a job to do. Purposeful discussion is used in planning, in enlightening and guiding, in answering questions and solving problems, in arriving at decisions, and in evaluating individual and group enterprises. Such discussion calls for clear interplay of ideas and real thinking together. Children can see the need for speakers to make their meaning clear and for listeners to give thoughtful attention in order to respond. A speaker may find his contribution challenged and be required to defend it or modify his point of view in order to help the group reach a satisfactory conclusion. If he feels he cannot modify his stand any further, he must decide what adjustment he can make to group needs and still hold his dissenting opinion.

Perhaps a group of children can evolve standards for participation similar to these:

> Have something to say.
> Say it clearly so others will understand what you mean.
> Speak in a clear, pleasant voice.
> Make your speech (usage) acceptable.
> Back your points with evidence from experience or authorities where necessary.
> Listen with an open mind to the ideas of others.
> Think through and weigh their contributions.
> Be willing to change your mind if evidence convinces you of the need for it.
> Be courteous at all times, even when you disagree.
> Give thought to the needs of the group as well as your own needs and interests.

With younger children, any discussion may resemble an experience meeting. Even older children frequently wander off into subthemes suggested by the discussion or enabling them to recount experiences that come to mind. When the purpose is sharing experiences, monologues delineating the experiences of individuals will predominate. But "lonestar" performances have no place in types of discussion which are designed to probe an area or to result in decisions or action unless an individual child happens to have become an authority in the area under discussion.

Every child needs to develop understanding of group processes, and some understanding can be achieved in the elementary school. The teacher of younger children almost invariably assumes the role of chairman or discussion leader. He may call children's attention to the necessity to hear everyone's ideas and to avoid monopolizing the discussion. He exerts the leadership necessary to draw out timid children and help aggressive ones learn consideration. As children are ready, he helps them acquire skill in leading a small group or in assuming responsibility for a portion of the class discussion. They can learn under guidance how to draw upon the knowledge and experience of the group, how to keep the discussion moving, how to summarize and draw material together at the end of the discussion, and how to plan for group action. They can learn the roles of chairman, recorder, and resource person. All such experience begins very simply with the teacher turning over to individuals bits of responsibility they appear ready to handle. Children need to be encouraged to stop now and then to ask, "How are we doing? Why did this move along well? Did everyone feel a part of the group? Was all that we discussed relevant to our purpose? Did we at any point become lost in irrelevant details? If so, how can we avoid the problem next time?"

As one listens to the rebellious charges hurled by modern young people of high school and college age at society in general and the schools in particular, it is clear that a large part of their bitter resentment stems from school experience in which they were treated as empty cups to be filled or as pawns to be manipulated. Now they are demanding to talk and be heard. Their cry is for dialogue, yet they are often all too willing to know only one side of a problem and cut off all expression of conflicting rights and opinions. Here is a generation of young people who have actually not been taught democratic processes in the schools. They have neither seen them in operation nor participated in them. They have never learned to take part in open-minded discussion, and they know little of its power to achieve or of its satisfactions. Their behavior should convince everyone that it is never too early to begin to teach children to participate in discussion and to do it in a manner appropriate to a democratic society. Such skill must be learned over a long period of time. Its relevance to the problems of today is unmistakably clear, and children can gain a deep sense of personal worth and power as they achieve it.

The content for class discussion comes from any subject or any activity within the scope of the school. As children progress through the elementary grades, they are pushing back horizons and operating in an expanding world of interests, ideas, and vicarious experiences. Outside of school, the mass media are a constant source of new material. In school, at least in the past, textbooks have been the main resource with children studying, answering questions, and giving back what they have found on the pages. In work like this, ignorance can go undetected and unchallenged. Many children are able to give back what they have read without understanding it. Through discussion, children can clarify points of vagueness or misconception, probe beneath the surface for deeper meaning, put concepts into perspective, and make the dead words on a page come to life. In short, they can bring new ideas out of the twilight into the sunlight of clear understanding. In the course of this, children can note how words may be used to distort or obscure meaning as well as how they can be marshaled to clarify meaning and express it accurately.

Discussion includes exposition. Children need innumerable opportunities to set forth their ideas in clear, organized fashion. Perhaps their first need for planning is in the daily sharing periods in the kindergarten and early grades. These are possibly the child's only opportunity to select what he wants to say, to present it to an audience, and note audience reaction. For the young child showing a new toy, the first dandelion of the season, or telling about an out-of-school experience, or the older child giving a talk on his hobby, his own reading, or exploration, it is his own personal moment as the center of attention. He should have any help he needs to build confidence in his ability to interest an audience and make his contributions increasingly valuable to his peers. In the course of this, children need to be encouraged to interact with each other, not just with the teacher. Criteria for evaluation should grow out of the children's experience as they work together and not be simply the teacher's criteria superimposed on the group.

Individual and group reports are an essential part of any social studies, science, or literature program. The content differs from subject to subject, but efforts to improve quality of exposition can be a consistent program from kindergarten to college if teachers are clear regarding their goals and sensitive to the needs of each individual. Discussion needs to be probing, exploratory, tentative, the kind that pushes back boundaries of experience rather than draws them tight.

From Dialogue to Monologue

Young children move from the realm of immediate, present experience to what is coming next, then to the past, and finally to what is outside actual experience. When they first begin to tell stories, their language becomes independent of present time and immediate experience. They may tell things imaginatively as they might be, not as they are. They learn to generalize and to project out into creatures or creations apart from themselves. They start with a small, close, and familiar audience and gradually learn to talk with unknown and finally with distant, unseen people as they must in writing. Telling stories may be done first through drawing, painting, and dramatizing, perhaps only later through language. For many deprived children, drama may be the most important creative medium since it demands less of language, and more can be communicated through expressive movement. In these children, language may be the last area in which confidence develops. Yet when they do use language spontaneously in their dramatic play, it is vivid, colorful, and highly expressive. It may, in fact, have far more concreteness, vitality, and richness than the language of children from more favored backgrounds.

American schools tend to do far less with drama than many English schools. John Dixon, in his report of the Dartmouth conference, "collects all the multifarious English activities under four headings: on the one hand, talk and drama; on the other, writing and reading."[5]

The language of books, of writing, differs from the language of moment-to-moment verbal interaction. Dixon feels that in learning to read, children are in danger of feeling "a sudden discontinuity," a change from familiar dialect forms which can set up a real linguistic barrier. He sees four stages through which children should move:

1. Much enjoyable listening to standard English—assimilating it with satisfaction through stories told by the teachers and later to her reading stories, too.
2. Reading aloud by the teacher and child of the child's own stories told in his own language and preserved in that form by the teacher who wrote them down.
3. Reading stories in standard English with accompanying talk.
4. Reading standard English on his own.[6]

Since learning to read and write leaves the child alone with language in a form that is new to him, each new activity should be preceded, accompanied, and followed by talk. Some teachers have in the past treated spoken English as if it were inferior to written English rather than a different form—a form children will gradually learn if they are allowed to grow into it without being forced. Forcing language growth of any kind appears to result in apathy and disinterest on the part of the learner.

On the other hand, teachers need to guard against underrating children's language abilities. Certainly, research in the language of elementary school children has found them using language far more advanced than the language of the books by which they are taught to read.[7]

Writing in the elementary school should begin not with assignment but with exploratory talk. It should be probing and tentative talk of the kind which pushes back the boundaries of thinking and opens many avenues without arriving at any patterned answers. It should encourage children to look into themselves for material and not to external rules and standards. Perhaps the standards are best established by the method Sybil Marshall has used with her class in England. She says:

> I would give them enough patterns, but not in the form of exercises. I would give them patterns in speech, in books, in poetry, and in plays. I would not subject my pupils to ten minutes a day under the ultraviolet lamp of intense grammatical exercises, but would instead seek out every patch of literary sunshine and see to it that the pupils worked and played in its warmth and light until grammatical usage and good style, the balance and cadence of sentences, and the happy choice of the most significant words soaked into them through every one of their senses. . . . It is much more important, surely, to be bursting with things to write about and not know precisely how to write them, than to know all the rules and not have anything to write.[8]

What the elementary school calls creative writing, in which children express their own ideas, feelings, and reactions, is perhaps the best of children's writing and that most closely related to their best use of oral language. Often it gives teachers insight into what goes on inside a child and why he responds as he does, perhaps even better than in his oral responses.

Oral language in the elementary school is both means and end. It is almost of necessity the stuff of which the entire curriculum is made if it is a curriculum that touches vitally the lives of children. Today, when speech is of the utmost significance in every aspect of life outside the school, nothing could be more relevant.

NOTES

1. Harold B. Allen, "Porro Unum Est Necessarium," in *NCTE Distinguished Lectures for 1969*. Champaign, Illinois: National Council of Teachers of English, 1969, pp. 98–99.

2. Herbert J. Muller, *The Uses of English*. New York: Holt, Rinehart and Winston, 1967, p. 107.

3. Otto Jesperson, *Mankind, Nation, and Individual from a Linguistic Point of View*. London: Allen and Unwin, 1946.

4. J. N. Britton, "Speech in the School" in *Some Aspects of Oracy*. NATE Bulletin, Vol. 11, No. 2, 1965, Birmingham, England, p. 23.

5. John Dixon, *Growth Through English*. Reading, England: National Association for the Teaching of English, 1967, p. 32.

6. Ibid., pp. 16 and 17.

7. Ruth G. Strickland, *The Language of Elementary School Children: Its Relationship to the Language of Reading Textbooks and the Quality of Reading of Selected Children*. Bulletin of the School of Education, Indiana University, Vol. 38, No. 4, July, 1962.

8. Quoted from *Experiment in Education* by Sybil Marshall in Muller, *The Uses of English*, p. 42.

On Improving the Speech of Children

JOHN W. BLACK

Regents Professor of Speech
The Ohio State University

You were not cast in the role of a teacher but successfully aspired to become one. There were probably many positive reinforcements along the way from friends, family, and your own teachers. Perhaps very early in life you were convinced that you possessed the appropriate personal traits for teaching. Children in the neighborhood by the names of Betty, Mary, Billy, and Jimmie (or names that you gave them as you played the role of a teacher) may have made up your first class. It became clear to you as you grew older that you wanted to teach, that you could hold interest, that you could maintain discipline, and that your *voice was appropriate*. Perhaps you were fortunate in being reared in a home in which speech was important. The examples and attitudes of your parents toward speech simply led the way to your own speech improvement. A progressive sequence of stages and aspects of speech improvement was a normal accompaniment to your achievement.

Your autobiography would probably include several special experiences that you remember. Perhaps many more influences among the events of your developmental years passed unnoticed. In directing these sentences to you, I am implying that your history of speech improvement and your present speech are inseparable from the task that confronts you for improving the speech of your pupils. Speech improvement appropriate to growth and maturation lies naturally in the background of achievement. Much of this improvement is unconscious, simply the absorption of the atmosphere of home, school, and community. The conviction that some points of view are important, that some social movements are important, and that the individual has an opinion that should be voiced to the relevant audience is a vital part of the kind of atmosphere that provides a natural climate for speech improvement from the earliest age.

Not all children grow up with opportunities to acquire verbal skills, nor have all of them shared with you an equal opportunity for professional achievement. Indeed they may even be turned off in their efforts to engage in meaningful communication. For example, in response to their first signs of inquisitiveness about familial relations to geography, they may curtly be informed that "your family has always lived on this river and always will." In such a response there seem to be no social issues that matter, no vocal inflections that have been practiced before audiences, no careful enunciation of phonemes, no intimation that speech is sometimes mirthful, and no reason to suppose that there are degrees of excellence between poor speech and that which you have acquired— the speech of a professional person.

As a teacher you have the opportunity to reinforce the child who brings good speech to school. This is at the same time both a strength and a weakness in our school system —for so long the better speaker has been called upon to represent the class, to recite the poems, and even to raise the flag. Speech improvement, however, is a basic need of the mirthless, the silent, the unintelligible, the timid, the child who gives no certain indication that he is hearing the teacher, let alone understanding him.

Speech Improvement in the Early Grades

Although there are many aspects of speech, it is not my intention to single out any one of them as being more important than the others in a program of speech improvement, unless it be motivation. For speech-deprived children, the special target of this essay, a reasonable substitute for motivation is fun. And speech-deprived children can have fun with a group activity devoted to voice stretching. It is convenient to think of the voice as having four dimensions: loudness, fundamental pitch, rate, and timbre. In the motivated voice of achievement, these four attributes blend in a variable sequence appropriate to the sense of the message. In the lifeless response, "Your family has always lived on this river," there is usually a monotonous wasting away of a scarcely audible initial syllable.

Thus, one trait of the target speech toward which you are leading your pupils is *vocal variability,* a documented characteristic of speech that is "preferred" by listeners in contrast to speech that is "less preferred." But before you can help your speech-deprived children attain vocal variability, you have first the not-so-easy task of eliciting speech, and, second, the task of helping them vary their speech in loudness, pitch, rate, and timbre. To accomplish these tasks, you must provide a context of fun for your pupils.

One teacher starts working with speech-deprived children by writing this sentence on the chalkboard: "Tom's b*a*ll *i*s r*e*d." She then extracts the vowels from the sentence, /ɑ, ɔ, ɪ, ɛ/, and conducts a number of verbal gymnastics with these four vowels. (The four symbols a, c, i, e and similar symbols will be used infrequently in this chapter; however, the meaning of each symbol is obvious and no knowledge of phonetics is essential for reading the exercises. I hope that you will master the rudiments of phonetics, if you have not done so already, to help you conduct a speech improvement program.)

After the teacher writes "Tom's ball is red" on the chalkboard and extracts the four vowels, she repeats the vowel sounds several times for memorization. The pupils speak the vowels in unison.

Next, the pupils repeat the vowels in unison, giving the final one an upward inflection. (Directly above the vowels written on the chalkboard, the teacher draws arrows pointing to the right and, in the case of the last vowel, diagonally upward.) Then, the pupils repeat the vowels, giving the final vowel a downward inflection. (The teacher draws another arrow on the chalkboard, pointing downward.) She continues with exercises with those four vowels:

1. The pupils repeat the vowels in unison in a low key or pitch.
2. The pupils repeat the vowels in unison in a high key.
3. The pupils repeat the vowels quite rapidly, in staccato fashion.
4. The pupils repeat the vowels with a pause between the first and second, the second and third, and so on.
5. The pupils repeat the vowels softly.
6. The pupils repeat the vowels loudly.
7. The pupils repeat the vowels first with increasing loudness and then with decreasing loudness.

Now come some crucial tests. Several of the children may have been making two vowel sounds instead of four. The collapsing of /ɑ, ɔ/ is a characteristic of many pronunciation dialects, especially of those dialects that do not accompany the language of achievement. Similarly, the collapsing of /ɪ, ɛ/ is frequent. Here, in the vowel play with four isolated vowels extracted from "Tom's ball is red," one has an opportunity to develop vowel quality and the uniqueness among vowels, without speaking directly of the pronunciation of words. The primary concern here is to help the child realize the range and potential of vocal variability.

To help pupils distinguish among vowel sounds and also to help them achieve vocal variability, you might perform additional exercises like these:

1. Repeat the four vowels in "Tom's ball is red" in an order like this, having pupils pronounce them in unison: /ɑ, ɑ, ɪ, ɪ/, /ɔ, ɔ, ɛ, ɛ/, and /ɑ, ɔ, ɪ, ɪ/.
2. Have pupils repeat the vowels in a tense voice and then in a full relaxed voice.
3. Have pupils imitate your repetition of the vowels in a nasal voice and an oral voice.

After you have completed those exercises, you may wish to return to the sentence, "Tom's ball is red." First, you speak the sentence as a positive statement and then as a question, having pupils repeat it after you. You also repeat the sentence, emphasizing various words and asking pupils to say the sentence in unison.

Tom's ball is red.
Tom's *ball* is red.
Tom's ball *is* red.
Tom's ball is *red*.

That same teacher who works for vocal variability through extensive choral repetitions of vowels as described above—and does so in a context of fun—also teaches children that some consonants are musical and some are nonmusical. Possibly the words musical and nonmusical are inconsequential, but the appraisal of experiences in making different consonants seems to be contributory toward vocal play, oral participation, and fun. That teacher performs exercises like these:

1. She leads the group in many rapid repetitions of the sound / t /.
2. She contrasts the / t / in *T*om's and the / d / in re*d*.
3. She practices sustaining and repeating these sounds: / m /, / l /, / r /.
4. She practices sustaining the sound / z / in Tom'*s* and i*s*.

This explanation borders on the tedious. The exercises, however, led by a motivated teacher, can generate a lot of speech production among speech-retarded children. The teacher writes the sentence that is used to generate vocal variety on the chalkboard. The teacher's gestures frequently relate the transient utterances to the more fixed written form of the sentence. Changes are made in a sentence. For example, the teacher might write: "Tom's ball is round." *Round* introduces the troublesome diphthong / au/. Many variants of this diphthong may be expected, ranging from / æ / of the Wabash River Valley to the triphthong / ɪ æ ə / farther south. (For obvious reasons, the children should practice the sound in isolation, not merely in the context of a cluster of phonemes that may turn out to be unintelligible.) Then the teacher substitutes *white* for *red* and interest focuses on the diphthong. If you substitute *tinfoil* for red, you may hear the fourth troublesome diphthong / ɔɪ / as / bɔɪl > bɔl / or as the medial sound of *bird* / ɝ / / bɔɪl > bɝl /.

The sole reason for this series of sustained exercises in isolated sounds is not to achieve phonetic accuracy. This is an objective, but only one of several. It is related to the exercises in "echolalia" that are exploited by Ruth Golden. Other objectives, however, as in her case, are also sought. The sentences change from time to time and the effect is similar to that of drills, much used in the teaching of languages. The teacher frequently turns to the sentences on the chalkboard; vowels, consonants, and diphthongs, although practiced in isolation, have an obvious verbal context and an orthographic representation. The audible repetitions of the voiceless plosive / t / relate to a word that is in view on the chalkboard. The speech-retarded child is stretching his oral production *in the context of language.* Hopefully, in turn, the language has some relevance to observed facts and events, as the following sentences, written on the chalkboard in February, have relevance:

> The valentine will be in the box.
> The valentines are in the box.
> The valentines were in the box.

You should pay special attention to, and construct exercises on, the use of prepositions. These are as troublesome to the speech-retarded child with normal hearing as they are to the deaf child; that is to say, they are baffling. The omission of some prepositions characterizes some poor speech; the substitution of prepositions, other speech.

Thus, the overall objectives of exercises that seem to

point to phonemic precision have much greater significance, including the learning of phonemic discrimination, an appreciation that phonemes occur in the context of language that can also be written and read visually, and also that phonemes occur in a standard syntax. The exercises also permit the matching of a well-spoken sentence —visible on the chalkboard—with an appropriate gesture on the part of the teacher. (The use of the gesture has not been discussed, but it seems sufficiently clear as a single statement.) Most of these procedures have been borrowed from one teacher; however, they bring together the practices of many workers who are trying to improve the speech of speech-deprived children.

The skills of speech production, present in the appropriately spoken message, are not the only linguistic needs of communication-deprived children. The exercises discussed above had a feature of repetition; the pupil may have been slow to make discriminations, but sooner or later he heard the essential distinctions. He must learn to communicate, however, in an environment in which one-time transmission is presumed. This is remote to a surprising number of children. For them, in a quasi-social communication environment, *huh* seems to be an audible— and expected—punctuation between successive renditions of the same message. These children need listening experiences. Probably they have never heard the children's stories that people who have achieved take for granted as an experience in growing up. Probably these children do not understand clearly the language of directions:

> Underscore one word.
> Cross out one word.
> Encircle one word.
> Fold your paper.

Needless to say, any listening exercises will be helpful. As schools become larger and as others are planned for specific populations, the hope becomes reasonable that a listening laboratory for children may become a reality. Such a laboratory could be beneficial to improvement in both listening and speaking. A language laboratory would facilitate the administering of sound-discrimination tests, ones that require the identification of a sound or ones that call for "same-different" responses. These tests are beneficial and feasible exercises in any classroom situation and should certainly be part of the materials of any teacher of speech improvement. A child might be induced to speak with considerable vocal variety—and with, for him, an unusual rhythm—if he is asked to repeat:

> "The time has come," the Walrus said,
> "To talk of many things:
> Of shoes—and ships—and sealing-wax—
> Of cabbages—and kings—
> And why the sea is boiling hot—
> And whether pigs have wings."

The foregoing procedures have largely ignored the original remarks of the child. These, however, are an anticipated product of the training process. You are not teaching a parent nor are you an indifferent listener, but you are a person who will be a contributing member in class discussions and in society. The parroting exercises above may have aided syntactic structures but surely do not insure acceptable syntax. The test comes in spontaneous oral behavior.

Brown and Bellugi, in reporting on children's acquisition of syntax, note that one common procedure followed by mothers is to expand the compressed speech of the child. The child has heard the full-dress version of his fragmentary utterance whether he chooses to repeat it or not. Some examples follow:

Child	Mother
Baby highchair	Baby is in the highchair.
Mommy eggnog	Mommy had her eggnog.
Eve lunch	Eve is having lunch.
Mommy sandwich	Mommy'll have a sandwich.
Sat wall	He sat on the wall.
Throw Daddy	Throw it to Daddy.
Pick glove	Pick the glove up.

The teacher may expect to follow a similar pattern with the speech-deficient child, not reprimanding him remark by remark, but only saying back to him what he has said, and saying it in acceptable syntax. Ruth Golden reports many instances of "compressed forms" among her students in the Detroit schools. An obvious procedure for the teacher is to use a set of listening and speaking exercises for a children's language laboratory. The teacher bent on improving the speech of his pupils can also expand the compressed utterances with full and complete vocalization, intonation, and emphasis.

"Sharing" seems to be a well-accepted part of the language arts program. A common difficulty is that some children want to do all the sharing while the timid ones hold back. Generally, our speech-improvement program is aimed at the timid, and one of the objectives is to achieve participation. Here, in participation, is spontaneous speech. Importantly, the sharing exercise is not divorced from the exercises in the remainder of our program. Perhaps a fragmentary sentence of a sharing report is expanded on the chalkboard after the report and the vowels and the consonants are treated in isolation.

Apart from such structured procedures for bringing about speech improvement among young children, the teacher has an important one at his control: the model of speech that he sets. It has been clearly shown that people are copycats in matters of speech. If one person in a conversation raises his voice, the other tends to raise his voice. If one person is repeating numerals that he is hearing from another, the repeater tends to group the numerals in the same way that he heard them. If a person is relaying messages that have an upward inflection, he tends to use an upward inflection in his repetition; similarly, downward inflections generate downward inflections. Slow speech on the part of one person generates slow speech on the part of the other, and, conversely, fast speech causes fast speech. A person in a conversation may find himself using considerably more variability in pitch than he usually does simply because he is talking with someone who is using an unusual number of upward and downward vocal inflections and ones of unusual extents. During the school year, the teacher delivers a very high proportion of the speech that is heard by the child. Whether he wishes it so or not, the child is copying this speech. Clearly, the teacher bears a marked responsibility.

The Need for Standard Speech

Throughout the discussion of the preceding section, the reasons for improvement and the nature of the target speech toward which the teacher aspires were topics scarcely raised. The young child is immersed in improving his language skills: comprehension, recognition of the vocabulary, reading, spelling, and the like. His oral abilities should develop concurrently. The only rationale for speech improvement that has been mentioned is that vocal variety has been demonstrated to be a preferable trait in the opinion of listeners. The only name that has been given the target speech is "the speech of achievement," and this has been presumed to be illustrated by the speech of the teacher. It behooves us, then, to look more closely at the reasons for speech improvement and at the character of the target speech than we have done thus far. In large measure, these two searches lead to the same reasoning.

In the words of J. B. Phillips, translator of the New Testament, Paul wrote to the Corinthians, "Unless you make intelligible sounds . . . how can anyone know what you are talking about?" Here is both a reason for speech improvement and a trait of the improved speech: intelligibility. This was a keystone to communication for Paul. It was probably on Shakespeare's mind day in and day out. Let us remember a singular scene in *Hamlet*. Hamlet's uncle has killed Hamlet's father and married Hamlet's mother. If Hamlet could be sure of all this, he would kill his uncle, now his stepfather; at least he thinks he would. A group of versatile traveling players has stopped at the castle, and Hamlet has written a speech for the principal actor to insert in a set play. Hamlet will watch his father's murderer, that is, his stepfather, and if he but winces, Hamlet will know where the guilt lies. The special lines are not enough; how they are said also matters. Hamlet coaches his actor:

> Speak the speech, I pray you, as I pronounced it to you, trippingly on the tongue. But if you mouth it, as many of your players do, I had as lief the town crier spoke my words.

Here is a plea: "I know you are capable of being intelligible. If you are otherwise, the lines will be meaningless, not understood. They might as well be spoken by the least intelligible persons in the experience of men who are now living, that is, by the town criers." Possibly, you too have known groups of individuals whose work typically was marked by unintelligible utterances: at one time or another chimney sweeps have fitted the mold, newspaper vendors, circus barkers, announcers of incoming and departing trains, auctioneers, and possibly personnel in some courtrooms. You can extend the list.

Shakespeare attributed unintelligibility to "mouthing the speech." There are many other causes, and each teacher is free to use his own language in describing them —slovenly enunciation, imprecise articulation, mumbling, and a host of other descriptive terms all of which point to a single effect: reduced intelligibility. The causes of this effect, however, are really more diverse and deep-rooted than the foregoing cluster of words about the speech mechanism would suggest. In fact, one of the most obvious causes, even to the most casual observer, is missed by this focus on the mouth and lips. This is speech of insufficient vocal intensity, or soft speech.

Unheard and misunderstood remarks, of course, are very expensive in the classroom. Time is spent as the class waits to learn whether or not a remark was really misunderstood; more time is spent in repeating the remark; and the outcome is that the exchange of guiding and helpful information is drastically reduced, sometimes by one-half. These are not the only costly results. A garbled and misunderstood message is accepted at face value, and the teacher or student is left remembering falsehoods.

Intelligibility is more than a classroom matter. It is a criterion of successful communication in conversations, public meetings, and matters of national defense. A warship is manned by personnel from our entire nation. The controlling nervous system of the ship is a telephone network to which these young men are assigned with no special regard to their facility in speech. Time in relaying messages is of the essence. There is no time for the listener to say "huh" and wait for a repeated and louder version of the same message that he failed to understand. Aircraft traveling at supersonic speeds do not accomodate many "syllables per mile." The first rendition of the exchange of messages between the pilot and the control tower must be mutually intelligible.

The implied dangers of unintelligibility within the scope of national defense lead us one step closer to the heart of the present discussion. During World War II, more than 2,000 officers-in-training were tested for intelligibility. They worked in groups of twelve, speaking for intelligibility tests in rotation; when they were not speaking, they served as listeners for their peers. Special note was taken of the region of origin of these young men, and the scores of speaking ability and of listening ability were studied in relation to these regions of origin, that is, the geographical regions in which the young men learned to talk. There was a considerable difference between one geographical group and another. On the average the most intelligible speakers—both to people of like origins and to others—came from "the region of Lake Michigan." The least intelligible speakers—again to their peers and to others—came from a large area conveniently called "the region of the Rio Grande." Midway between these two extremes lay the speech of "the Deep South." A rationale, then, for both speech improvement and the target speech lies in intelligibility.

It may be convenient in some circumstances to continue to use the coined phrase "speech of achievement." It does imply an upward movement on the part of an individual, symbolic of an upward mobility on the part of a segment of society. This principle was once caught and exploited in the Horatio Alger stories for boys of junior high school age. It has been captured for other youth in "short biographies of successful men." Perhaps it was repeated for older people with "the history of psychology through autobiography." Records of this upward mobility among American society abound. Into each instance, one can read a progression to the speech of achievement—and as achievement is a will-of-the-wisp that seems to dart and jump on and beyond, just so is speech improvement a continuing process.

Isn't it time for us to call this target speech "standard speech"? There may be minor disagreements about the description of standard speech. There may even be times when the standard seems to fluctuate from the speech of the university classroom to that of some rather bizarre locales. I do not want to equate standard speech with standard pronunciation. Yet a popular dictionary has carried for several decades a helpful sentence about the latter which may have some bearing upon the former: "The standard of English pronunciation, so far as a standard may be said to exist, is the usage that now prevails among the educated and cultured people to whom the language is vernacular." In the uneven developments of history, nonetheless, there are many times and circumstances when the role of the speech of the "educated and cultured people" might be questioned. There will always be these crosscurrents and undertows that alter the principal criteria for upward mobility and the achievement of a satisfying status in society.

Standard speech embodies vocal variety. It is characterized by intelligibility. Although it conveys the enthusiasms and the warmth of the talker and permits many generalizations about him, standard speech does not interfere with his anonymity. He may be marked as being from the United States or from another English-speaking country, as probably being from New England or from the Deep South, but the speaker can preserve a lot of his anonymity even though a broad pronunciation dialect is apparent. Subcultures within these categories need not be disclosed. One scholar puts it thus:

> I am not referring to standard English that may have with it a peculiar accent that can readily be identified with a certain section of the United States; I am referring to substandard English that can be readily identified as being a part of a culture within the large culture. When this happens there is a need for a change.

He justifies his conclusion thus:

> It is well known that most supermarket and dime store managers, for example, are reluctant to hire people who may have difficulty communicating with others.

These subcultures are numerous and of different kinds. Some of them, old ones, are easy to describe: they are geographical and may relate to early settlers, immigration, and migration. The Middle West is identified with a General American dialect; yet there are pockets of "foreign brogue" here and there, for example, longlived ones of German in Ohio. Also, much of the northern part of Ohio was awarded to New England war veterans. The result is apparent in the architecture, churches, and speech. One phonetician has drawn a crude line across Ohio, Indiana, and Illinois with Route 40. He posits one pronunciation dialect (subculture) below this crude dividing line and another above it. The path that Lincoln trod northward along the Wabash River and westward into

Illinois was followed by countless other migrants, many of whom stayed to live along the route. Personally, I remember a country church, perhaps thirty miles north of Route 40, founded by the settlers and named Old Kentuck.

The odd pronunciations of subcultural groups are as old as speech; yet they have always disclosed something about the speaker which he would like to preserve in anonymity. There is the classical account in Judges (12:6):

> They said to him, 'Shibboleth,' and he said, 'Sibboleth,' for he could not pronounce it right; then they seized him and slew him at the fords of Jordan and there fell at that time forty two thousand of the Ephriamites.

This was in 1150 B.C. The two subcultures spoke the same language and were divided by a mythical Route 40. More than a thousand years later the regional dialect of a subculture was recorded in a Christian episode. While Jesus was on trial, Peter was in the courtyard outside. He denied any knowledge of Jesus. Twice he defended himself against the charges of the maid. His Galilean, subcultural dialect gave him away, and the third accusation was telling:

> After a little while, the bystanders came up and said to Peter, 'Certainly you are one of them; for your accent betrays you' (Matthew 26:73).

There have been a number of other documented instances in which the pronunciation patterns of subcultural groups were used for identifying the "haves" and "have nots." You may use your own terminology for describing this aspect of language behavior and for relating it to reasons for modifying one's speech and to the desirable characteristics of standard speech. I am content to let it rest as "the preservation of personal anonymity" insofar as the unlocking of that anonymity would establish unimportant substantive barriers to communication, including diversionary ones and reduced intelligibility.

Improving Speech of Older Children

A lengthy discussion on the need for standard speech may be superfluous for the older school child who is willing to set about zestfully to improve his speech. However, in spite of his eagerness—if Lenneberg is correct—time is running out for him. With each additional year of maturation, the speech patterns of the student become more firmly imbedded. Lenneberg has hypothesized that with puberty the period of language readiness comes to an end, and that henceforth any changes in the individual's system of language are wrought with great difficulty. Moreover, apart from Lenneberg, with maturation an identity develops between a person's manner of speech and his feeling of personal identity. Well-intentioned criticisms of a person's speech may lead to improved performance or, equally notable, may be received almost as though they are personal attacks.

The child may speak a different language at home and with his playmates; it serves his fun functions—games, anecdotes, and life at the social center. The "district school English" may be but useless impedimenta. Thus, in addition to the motivation that the teacher can provide, the child will need patience and determination, as well as zest. Although nothing can be substituted for the motivating influence of the teacher and her enthusiasm for improving speech, the foregoing suggestions may be helpful for working with the taciturn child or even the normal one.

The discussion has led us through three desirable traits

of all speech. Yet the generalization "all speech" is a tremendous one; at the very least, it extends from the colloquial give-and-take among neighbors through the formal presentation of platform address, and neither of these poles is stable. There are degrees of informality in conversation and degrees of formality in public address. One beneficial exploration of speech habits in New York City examined speech in casual speech, careful speech, reading style (contextual), word lists, and minimal pairs. The experimental subjects were categorized roughly according to economic status: lower class, working class, lower middle class, and upper middle class. Irrespective of the deviation from standard speech that was under observation, the deviations were progressively less noticeable as the experimental subjects gave examples of casual speech, careful speech, reading style (contextual), word lists, and minimal pairs. One might say that speech improved from one style to the next. Also, irrespective of the group that was under observation, fewer deviations tended to occur with the higher economic classes and more deviations with the lower economic classes. Importantly, among young people from eight to twenty-three years of age, progressively fewer errors were made by the older ones than by the younger ones. There were five indices that were generalized to be important in the description of standard English speech (pronunciation) in New York City:

1. The use of *r* in post-vocalic and pre-consonantal positions, as in *guard* and *horse*.
2. The vowel in *dad, ask, dance, had,* and *cash*.
3. The stressed vowel in *awful, coffee,* and *office* (the frequent collapsing of this vowel with / ɑ / has been mentioned earlier in the discussion.

4. The use of / θ / in *thing* and *thin*.
5. The use of / ʏ / in *then* and *the*.

The teacher in a community or urban school who has to make up his own list of singular distortions that mar standard speech bears a terrific responsibility, for one or two pet grievances may become overworked while other equally important deviations are slighted. In fact, like speech improvement itself, this task of framing the salient features of a region's standard and substandard speech may become a progressive year-on-year task.

One criterion among many used for the detection of substandard speech is the fact that idiosyncrasies are reflected in unacceptable forms in writing, perhaps in spelling or in syntax. Some teachers have gone so far as to establish that they can name the subcultural group to which a writer of a high school theme belongs. The traditional rules of writing are sufficiently rigid that many deviations from standard are readily designated *errors*. This is less the case with speaking than with writing; yet the clear matching of an obvious error in writing with a similar pattern in speaking seems adequate cause to name the latter substandard.

There are many approaches to the older school child whose speech a teacher would hope to improve. One is to appeal to the boys in terms of their prowess with their bodies, their muscles. The age of sports is upon them; they are eager to excel in the race, in the jump, and in the distance the ball is thrown. With or without the coach's help, the teacher of speech improvement can explain that every aspect of talking is "muscle business":

1. The loud voice comes with the rapid contraction of the muscles of the abdomen.
2. Variable pitch comes with the rapid manipulations of the muscles of the larynx.

3. Precisely spoken consonants result from the minutely and exactly controlled muscles of articulation.
4. Differentiation of vowels comes with the coordinated control of the mandible, the tongue, and the lips.
5. The turning *on* of nasality with / m, n, ŋ, /, and the turning *off* of nasality with the other sounds, comes with the muscularly driven closing and opening of the pharyngeal port to the nasal passage.

All of these muscles must be exercised and must respond in a manner that is every bit as coordinated as the batter's sweep with the bat that connects with the well-hit ball. Practice is essential for all activities that are muscle business.

A second approach that works with many older students is the intelligibility test. This procedure yields a result that will not be denied; the talker, whatever his age, will be convinced that there is a fault in communicating, and more importantly that it lies with him. In its first form, as used in schoolrooms, the intelligibility test was made up of obscure words of English, drawn heavily from Shakespeare. Each of several speakers read one of twenty separate lists of these words to panels of their peers who sat in armchairs at the rear of the room, thirty to forty feet removed from the speaker and sitting at right angles to the direction the speaker was facing. Thus, the speaker would read *scythe,* and the panel of twelve to twenty listeners would be expected to write what they heard. Some of the students would, of course, write *sigh,* some *sign,* and some merely *I.* Nevertheless, the sets of responses to the list read by each speaker were put into a single envelope (each speaker had read the target words as printed on the face of his envelope). He would then compare the written responses of his peers with what he had tried to say, for example, *scythe.* It was a humiliating experience, but a convincing one. He was simply unintelligible to his classmates, who were sitting a reasonable distance from him.

Obviously, the procedure described in the foregoing paragraph could lead—and did lead—to an intelligibility score. In this instance, it was a score of the speaking ability (intelligibility) of an individual. In other circumstances, the tests can be used to measure the lines of communication between talkers and listeners or used to measure the listening ability of individuals. At present, however, we are concerned with the intelligibility of youthful talkers of school age.

The intelligibility testing procedure has been considerably refined in the last half century. One test that carries considerable prestige is called the "phonetically balanced test." This is a series of lists of English monosyllables, and the types of consonants—plosives, fricatives, and the like —are equally distributed among the lists. Each word is made up of three sounds—a consonant plus a vowel plus a consonant. These "PB lists" are readily available. The words can be scrambled from usage to usage and successive readings can be conducted in the manner of the test described above.

Another test with which I happen to be identified is a multiple-choice intelligibility test developed from a procedure similar to that described above. In developing the test, it became apparent that listeners tended to make the same errors; therefore, the test word and the three most frequent errors were grouped in a single-response set. A listener can make no other response than to cross out one of four words that appear in a group on his answer sheet. This test, distributed by Interstate Printers (Danville, Illinois), provides essentially a self-scoring intelligibility test—provided the teacher assembles a group of approximately twelve students who will cooperate with one another in taking the test. The administration of the test requires approximately twenty–five minutes; it can be administered to two groups of twelve students at the same time.

A student's score on the intelligibility test and the fact that two, three, or four of eleven listeners misheard a spoken word are convincing evidence to the older school child. No single exercise in my experience has brought more noticeable changes in the speech behavior of relatively self-satisfied students than the challenging exercise offered by intelligibility tests.

Third, reference has been made in an earlier portion of this discussion to the possible use of a language laboratory. These laboratories offer a number of possibilities that have not been available previously to teachers of speech. One intriguing possibility is "the tape loop," in which a single phrase, or a combination of phrases, sentences, and the like can be played over and over with perfect duplication. In the typical classroom approach to problems of language correction the teacher says a phrase and the student repeats it. The tape loop breaks this pattern by providing a predictable sequence of short silence, phrase, short silence, phrase, and so forth endlessly. The student might ask himself, why not repeat the phrase *with* the model? This can be fun. Many students experience what they report as "being in tune," or "sounding as though I am singing in a choir." The validity of the matching of the student's response with the taped stimulus is open to question. Nonetheless, the student believes that he has achieved a remarkable degree of similarity with the stimulus. This is something of which he is never quite sure as he repeats the teacher's model. It is of course more stimulating to him to be his own monitor of success than simply to receive an approving nod for having made a successful rendition of the teacher's model. The language laboratory, with the tape loop, offers possibility for speech improvement that is specific to the equipment. There are also many other opportunities available in the language laboratory to the teacher who is willing to search for ways to help children improve their speech.

Finally, I turn back to a topic of the first section: speech improvement should be fun. I have found that even parents can enjoy learning that their talk is "funny" and that college students can enjoy learning that they are not talking "English universal." High school students, too, have shown enthusiasm for lessons in speech improvement when they are given in a context of fun.

I have used such works as "John Davenport's Slurvian Self-taught" and dialect poems by James Russell Lowell and James Whitcomb Riley. I also use Kin Hubbard's "A Line a Day," which he wrote under the pseudonym Abe Martin. I use dialect poems, passages from novels, and newspaper columns as an exercise to stretch the voice of the older school child and to make him aware of various pronunciation dialects, including his own.

I would urge again and again that with many students the logical argument that unintelligibility is the student's own fault, although convincing, is futile. The reward comes with fun. There are many sources of fun with speech, but the most readily accessible lies in recorded versions of pronunciation dialects. These are sometimes disparaged as "eye dialects," to be distinguished from the real acoustic experience of a dialect. But the eye of the teacher, the eye of the alert child, and the well-written page can bring forth an acoustic dialect that is not the child's normal one. He can then reread the dialect he has spoken in standard English or in the "most formal public platform address." The experience, entertaining to his peers and new to himself, provides insightful learning.

All of us are familiar with "truths": speech is learned from the mother; speech is picked up from the peers; speech will take care of itself. These truths the teacher cannot believe, largely because speech seems to be an individual matter for each child. Some children don't talk; some utter incomprehensible phrases; some are garrulous. The range is infinite. During an important period prior to alleged closure of the language-learning period, the teacher is an authority figure with many school children. With the younger ones, the teacher can have an immediate effect on eliciting speech, shaping syntax, and, in short, improving speech. Here seems to be no necessity to reason why. With older children, the teacher may face a more difficult task. Some may ask, "Why should I change my speech?" I hope the essay has provided some answers. And in terms of methodology, I hope the chapter has emphasized that speech improvement is more likely to occur in a climate of fun.

REFERENCES

Brown, Charles T., and Charles Van Riper. *Speech and Man.* Englewood Cliffs, New Jersey: Prentice-Hall, 1966. The two authors have brought together an inspirational booklet on man in relation to his greatest achievement—speech. They are factual (perhaps you will find them dull during the first chapter or so); they are purposeful; they have fun. Surely within this mixture of experiences on the part of the authors, the teacher of speech improvement can find benefit. Indeed he may approach the discussion from the point of view of therapy (Van Riper) or from the point of general communication

(Brown). In any event, he will find the pages entertaining and worthwhile.

Byrne, Margaret C. *The Child Speaks.* New York: Harper & Row, 1965. The emphasis in this "speech improvement program for kindergarten and first grade" is on consonant sounds. Dr. Byrne puts in action the emphasis of this essay, *fun.* She provides interesting animal stories for the teacher to read. These, in turn, are loaded with selected consonant sounds. Here is an anthology with many good exercises.

Golden, Ruth I. *Improving Patterns of Language Usage.* Detroit: Wayne State University Press, 1960. The author sensed the teaching problem, took time off to study it, worked out partial solutions, and recorded them in this remarkable book. Mrs. Golden is Caucasian; she is engrossed in the language problems of Negro children in Detroit, and it has become eminently clear that she is accepted by the children and that her recommendations are standard. The bit-by-bit analysis of substandard Detroit speech should be studied by every teacher who is attempting to improve speech in the inner city.

Malmstrom, Jean, and Annabel Ashley. *Dialects U. S. A.* Champaign, Illinois: National Council of Teachers of English, 1963. This is the beginning of a book that should be expanded and brought up to date annually. It does much to expand many readers' notions of the word *dialect,* although it would satisfy no speaker or teacher of Italian or Spanish or any other true language *dialect.* Its final seven-page chapter, "Dialect and Literature," is especially helpful. Here is an easily accessible and authentic list of novels, short stories, poems, and plays that are representative of particular American pronunciation dialects.

Shuy, Roger W., ed. *Social Dialects and Language Learning.* Champaign, Illinois: National Council of Teachers of English, 1964. This is a discussion of the papers read at a conference on social dialects sponsored by the Office of Education. The participants were predominantly linguists. The teacher of speech improvement will benefit from almost all of the pages and particularly from the contribution of William Labov. He describes an in-process study of the speech of different socio-economic groups of New York City. One aspect of this report is singularly bothersome to me. In my discussion I have placed emphasis on fun experience and role playing but Labov reports instances in which the participants in New York City were apparently unaware that they were changing their voices as they imitated different people in their stories. This phenomenon, of course, needs to be studied. If voice stretching occurs unconsciously —and has no effect on conscious speech—then the teacher of speech improvement will have to reassess his position.

Wise, Claude M., *Introduction to Phonetics*. Englewood Cliffs, New Jersey: Prentice-Hall, 1958. The present essay has used several phonetic symbols, and, except possibly for / θ / in *thumb* and the / ɤ / in *though*, they have been self-explanatory. Wise's book deserves careful reading. I am tempted to say that "the smaller the print in his book, the more careful the reading should be." He astonishes us with some "recommended" pronunciations of words (these recommendations, of course, we shall not hurriedly pass on to the students; rather, we shall only introduce them subtly into our discussions). I can vouch for almost every hayseed pronunciation indicated on page 204. My experiences come from Fountain County, Indiana. I can also attest to the use, not necessarily dominant use, of many of these pronunciations there in 1970.

On Teaching Drama

GERALDINE BRAIN SIKS

Professor of Drama
University of Washington

Drama is natural to a child. Almost every child becomes absorbed in his own exciting, imaginative dramas as he represents life through action and impersonation in "dramatic play." Every child interacts continually with people and things, with his own thoughts and feelings, and, because of his many perceptions and a need to comprehend and organize life for himself, he is inclined to act out his many wonderings, curiosities, desires and conflicts. The human capacity to perceive, imagine, make believe, impersonate, interact, struggle with conflicts, and experience life in reflection provides the essential base of the art of drama.

To many adults, drama means only theatre. However, other adults, particularly those concerned with drama in education, view drama as a far broader discipline. During the last decade, elementary school teachers and college professors have attempted to revise existing courses of study, or design new curricula, for speech and drama in the elementary school. For both the revisions and the new programs, these four critical questions had to be answered:

1. Why teach drama to children?

2. What can be done to make drama and speech a central part of the educational program?
3. What should be taught to children as a part of the drama program?
4. How should it be taught?

The inclusion of creative dramatics in school programs began in 1925 when Winifred Ward introduced the term "creative dramatics" in a course for teachers at Northwestern University. Since then, courses for elementary teachers have been included in training programs in several colleges and universities. Classes in creative dramatics have also been included as leisure-time activities in many recreational programs for children, but they have remained on the periphery in public school education in elementary and junior high schools.

In *Playmaking with Children* Miss Ward noted four widely different attitudes toward the use of dramatics in education. First, some educators looked upon dramatics as a tool for learning facts. Second, others thought of it purely as recreation not at all concerned with education. Third, still others looked upon creative dramatics only as therapy. And fourth, some regarded it as an art with such unquestioned value that they believed it should be a part of every elementary school curriculum on equal footing with music and the graphic and plastic arts. It is necessary at this point to indicate that creative dramatics will probably continue to serve those four purposes, and interested teachers will find considerable literature in the field suggesting guidelines for sharing creative dramatics with children.

An emerging national attitude in drama education indicates that drama should be taught to children as an art in its own right. It will then be more effective as a method, therapy, or recreation. In this essay we will present that point of view, seeking to answer the four questions we posed at the outset. The first is, as you recall: Why teach drama to children?

We believe that the aim of drama in education is fundamentally the same as the aim of all childhood education, that is, to assist a child's development and learning. If education is regarded as a process of changing behavior, education in drama aims primarily to effect change in a child's processes of behavior in the broad sense of modifying his thinking, feeling, and doing as he interacts with life. In essence, a child's experiences in learning drama will seek to change his natural, spontaneous, and impulsive behavior, evident in his perceptions and representations of life in his dramatic play, to more consciously controlled, imaginative behavior required both to do drama with other children and to interact with life. This means that a child's processes of thinking, feeling, and doing will be educated in his involvement in the activity of learning drama with his peers. More specifically, the objectives of drama in the elementary school include the following: (1) to begin to develop a child's cognitive skills and abilities required to do drama in the related roles of a player (actor), playmaker, and designer-producer; (2) to foster the development of a child's affective abilities by involving him in experiences in which he begins to discover and enjoy dramatic form as an audience and to make discoveries about human values and the relationship of drama to real life experiences; and (3) to guide the child to acquire a body of knowledge through oral discourse in imaginative, dramatic processes with others so that his knowledge remains active and at his command. Although these objectives are admittedly ambitious, they focus toward one clear end: to teach the art of drama in relationship to a child's natural processes of learning—to assist his learning and developmental growth. Learning drama from this view should assist a child to develop as an imaginative, perceptive citizen, responsive and responsible to his society, his environment, and himself.

Underlying this fundamental aim are three premises. First, the art of drama is central to a child's understanding of life because the content of drama focuses on a child's natural processes of learning in relationship to his perceptions of human relationships and interactions with the environment. Second, dramatic interaction of persons involved in the active process of creation of the art is a primary vehicle for developing thought and language and engendering a variety of speech and oral language activity. Third, the instinctive, freewheeling behavior of the child can be changed to more self-controlled, imaginative, thinking behavior if the art of drama is taught from a process-activity point of view.

Our second question asks: What can be done to make drama and speech a central part of the educational program? From a realistic point of view, it appears that drama and speech will be emphasized only if drama is programmed as a central art in the existing framework of public school education in the English language arts curriculum. This thesis, proposed and advanced by James Moffett in *Drama: What Is Happening*, contends that "drama and speech are central to a language curriculum, not peripheral. They are base and essence, not specialties. I see drama as the matrix of all language activities, subsuming speech and engendering the varieties of writing and reading." This thesis rests on the assumption that dramatic interaction—doing things verbally in situations with other people—is the primary vehicle for developing thought and language. Moffett believes that a person learns language, literature, and composition in a "coherent way by participating in the experience of creating discourse: writing plays and short stories, poems and other forms; or acting, interpreting and creating drama in diverse and realistic situations."

Moffett's thesis implies a need for educators to recognize the noticeable amount of positive transfer from drama training to the actuality of living. This transfer is apparently influenced by several factors, chiefly drama's commonality with life. In a systematic drama program, a child is guided to experience and to solve human problems in innumerable situations that he is likely to encounter in real life. Another contributing factor in the transfer of training from drama to real life is the emphasis placed in drama education on problem solving. The problems children grapple with in learning drama are, in fact, problems they will face in their own environment—problems of human interaction and struggle for adjustment. In a systematic program, the content of drama at the outset is drawn from children's experiences with life rather than from literature. However, as the program develops and children learn fundamentals of drama and acquire behaviors essential to the perception, imagination, and improvisation, they are then introduced to the processes of interpretation, collaboration, and communication of dramatic literature. The substance of drama activities arises out of children's experiences with the physical environment, with other human beings, with ideas, and with themselves. And these are, of course, the major concepts of the art of drama. In a long-range program, children are guided to understand that their interactions and adjustments with their environment are fundamentally the same as those of all persons.

The children's learning of concepts is interwoven with

their use of language and with their acquisition of language skills. As language is used in simulated life experiences, a child acquires gradually the means of expressing relationships among concepts. Learning language in the ambience of drama contributes not only to the development of a child's abilities to think and to imagine but also to his use of language as a means of interaction with his environment. A child needs experiences daily, or at least twice a week, in which he is guided in a systematic order to interact verbally in drama situations with other children as they also learn to struggle and to adjust in human confrontations. For the most part in public shool education, there is at present no subject in the elementary curriculum that is organized systematically to provide education of this nature. This new view of the art of drama should prove valid in offering education in which learning contributes to the child's development of thought and speech processes and to his use of knowledge in relationship to living.

When children become involved in the pleasure of learning drama, they learn language by using it functionally in several fundamental operations. Children learn to think, to speak, to interact, and to communicate. They learn to use language actively in relation to experiences in group processes in forming drama. Improvisation calls for spontaneous thinking in situations involving interaction between people. Often, improvisational acting calls for different levels of thought at the same time; decisions have to be made spontaneously. What is required during improvisational acting is the ability to think within a situation; the ability to appraise a situation; the ability to think and to speak in order to adapt to a changing situation in relationship to the thinking, appraising, adapting, acting, and speaking of another person. Gradually, children learn to observe closely, particularly with their senses of sight and hearing. They develop an ability to observe the actions of a person with whom they act and interact; they also learn to observe the environment and to identify human reactions—both in the real and in the stage environment. Children gradually develop an ability to concentrate—to give complete attention while listening. Fluency and flexibility of thinking and speaking are exercised whenever a child operates in an imagined setting and situation in the role of another person or character. A child exercises his thinking whenever he aims to achieve a character's purpose in a face-to-face relationship with another person who, in a character role, opposes his purpose.

Because much of the experience in drama involves speaking, children exercise a flow of intelligent speech in a variety of operational modes, including soliloquy, monologue, dialogue, and discussion preceding and following the solving of problems. In a systematic program, drama activity serves to motivate children to read literature for several different purposes. For example, children may be encouraged to read about, to discover, and to describe dramatic situations for acting; to identify and relate to others incidents of conflict and resolution that may serve to suggest ways of solving dramatic problems of their own making; to identify opposing objectives in character relationships and to consider justifications of actions; to discover and use different modes of verbal interaction in original situations; and to read for the pleasure of discovering in literature imagined settings, character relationships, conflicts, and resolutions.

Similarly, drama serves to motivate children to write. For example, children are often stirred by exciting dramatic experiences to respond in various written forms. Children have been motivated to describe an imagined setting in detail, to write detailed biographical descriptions of main characters involved in the conflict, to offer an alternative motive and justification for a character who is trying to solve a problem, and to write dialogue to build a climax or resolve a conflict which has become stalemated in improvisation. Some children have even become so excited by experiences in drama that they write scenarios or entire plays in dramatic form.

In suggesting a practical way to include drama in the existing elementary school curriculum of public school education, it seems obvious that the educational values resulting from drama and language will benefit the child only by continuous and sequential experiences in learning drama. On the one hand, it appears that drama may be programmed in an elementary school curriculum as a fine art, a discipline in its own right only if there is time for it to be programmed on a regular basis. On the other hand, if there is no time to include drama as an art in an already crowded curriculum, it appears that it should be programmed as the matrix of the English language arts curriculum and taught regularly in each grade level from kindergarten through the sixth grade.

In attempting to explain how drama might become central in education, we have indicated some answers to the third question: What should be taught to children as a part of the drama program? If drama is to be taught as an art, it is important for every teacher to identify what the art of drama is. The teacher needs to understand both art and drama, and we assume that he does. We will simply add here that art is man's process of fashioning his perception of a basic human truth in a form which is universally recognized and understood and which arouses feelings and thought in others; and, the art of drama is formed by an imagining and imitating of characters involved in dramatic action that reflects an action of life.

It is our view that when the art of drama is treated as such fundamentally, it provides both a comprehensive and unified basis for study and creation. In *The Idea of a Theatre*, Francis Fergusson advances this premise by pointing out that the "notion of action and the imitation of action is the connecting link between the art of the dramatist and the interpretative art of the actor." Fergusson advocates that when "we directly perceive the action which the artist intends, we can understand the objectivity of his vision, however he arrived at it; and thence the form of his art itself. And only on this basis can one grasp the analogies between acting and playwriting, between various forms of drama, and between drama and other arts."

Our concern is with the process of forming or creating drama so that we may involve children in these processes. We must therefore clarify the basic elements which always prevail to give structure to the art when it reaches the collaborative process of performance for an audience. Whenever a performance becomes a living drama for an audience, the cardinal elements that interrelate to form the creation include the play, the players, the stagers, and the audience. This interrelationship of elements is based on two essential principles: first, a living drama depends on a group collaboration to produce a play; second, the actor is the focal point of the group collaboration.

The first principle calls for the collaboration of several arts into one single medium. These include the arts of literature, acting, directing, and staging. To combine and synthesize these arts, the cooperation of several artists is required, including primarily the playwright, the actor, and the stagers. In the group endeavor, each participant exercises his creative process for one clear aim—forming and performing a living drama for a living audience.

The second essential principle poses a question: Why is the actor the focal point of the dramatic production? If we refer to our definition of drama as an imagining and imitating of an action of life, we recognize that it is the actor who imitates the action of the play. Further, if we consider the question historically, we realize that drama did not develop out of the written play but rather that the written play developed out of the acting. The first playwright was indeed the player, the actor, the imitator of life.

In this approach to teaching drama, the drama curriculum becomes the structure designed to teach the art to children. On the one hand, the curriculum is structured to relate learning in drama to the developmental characteristics of children. On the other hand, the curriculum aims to develop the pupils' understanding of the structure of drama in a mode that is honest and accurate to the broad discipline of the art of drama. Thus, the curriculum presents content and learning activities in a manner that can be recognized as drama by a dramatist, an actor, a theatre designer, or director. In other words, the curriculum is designed to present the art to a child at the elementary level in a form which is true to the discipline at more advanced levels.

The content of the curriculum revolves around the four major elements of the art of drama: acting, audience, playmaking, and designing-producing the play. However, the actor-audience relationship is the essential core of this art, and thus the core of the drama program with children. Acting is emphasized centrally throughout the program with the audience element pervading all learning.

The elements of playmaking and designing-producing are learned in relationship to the core as a continuing development of the dramatic form toward its maturity—the collaboration of a synthesized whole into a living drama that is communicated to a peer audience. Thus, the program aims to teach children the elements of drama by relating each to the central element of acting.

While each artist in drama creates in his own individual manner, there are fundamental creative processes common to each: (1) perception, (2) imagination, (3) improvisation, (4) interpretation, (5) collaboration, and (6) communication. Each is a cognitive process used by a child in his natural mode of learning, and each provides a valid means for a child to learn a basic principle of the element of acting through active experiences. These processes as employed in this view of drama education are clarified briefly:

1. Perception is the process of discriminating among stimuli and of interpreting their meanings. It intervenes between sensory processes, on the one hand, and behavior, on the other. Being an intervening process, it is not directly observable. It can be investigated and understood only by observing behavioral responses made to stimuli under various conditions. For example, perceiving may be as simple a process as that of a child identifying by naming a body part, or it may involve a much more complex process as that of a child identifying and interpreting by describing and/or acting with others the meaning of a story or play.

2. Imagination is the process of forming mental images of what is not actually present to the senses. It may involve the process of forming mental images of what

has never been actually experienced or of creating new images or ideas by combining previous experiences.

3. Improvisation is the process of extemporizing physical actions (including speech) on the spur of the moment without previous preparation or rehearsal. Improvisation implies a process of making believe by imitation of actions or "acting like", a process not of exact correspondence in the imitation of an action but of a likeness. It is a process of perceiving, imagining, and creating a likeness or an essence of the physical actions of that character which is being imagined in a given circumstance. For example, in impersonation a child improvises frequently by imitating spontaneously a characteristic action, speech, or mannerism of a parent.

4. Interpretation is the process of perceiving and imagining to analyze and act out the intended meaning of an imagined character in a given circumstance, story, or play. The child acts in relationship to his individual perception and imagination and in relationship to the acting of another or others involved in the situation.

5. Collaboration is the process in which individuals cooperate by working together in a group endeavor aimed to synthesize individual interpretations into a play performed for an audience of peers.

6. Communication is the process in which individuals collaborate to synthesize a theatre production to impart thought, feeling, and the message of a play to an audience.

The drama program, structured in the nature of a spiral curriculum, develops in sequential progression through four phases. Phase One emphasizes the processes of *perception-imagination-improvisation*. Activities are designed to involve the child in learning basic acting principles as he applies them in using these essential processes. Phase Two emphasizes interpretation. Activities are designed to involve the child in applying the principles learned in Phase One to the process of interpretation of character in improvised story-playing. Phase Three emphasizes collaboration. Activities are designed to involve the child in applying the principles of collaboration in improvised story dramatization. Phase Four emphasizes communication. Activities involve the child in the process of collaboration with his peers to produce a scripted play and communicate its meaning in a performance for an audience of peers. On the one hand, if drama is included centrally as an art in an English language arts curriculum, it is assumed that the emphasis in kindergarten through second grade will be on the processes in Phase One. Phase Two would probably be emphasized in grade three; Phase Three in grade four; and Phase Four in grades five and six. On the other hand, at whatever grade level drama is introduced, a child needs to learn to apply basic acting principles with a degree of mastery in the processes of Phase One before he is prepared to move to the following sequential phases.

As explained, the curriculum aims to employ a process-activity program in which fundamental principles of drama will be learned by the child through innumerable activities that involve him in the essential processes of doing drama. Thus, a child learns drama by doing it. As Jerome Bruner explained in *The Process of Education*, "Grasping the structure of a subject is understanding it in a way that permits many other things to be related to it meaningfully. To learn structure, in short, is to learn how things are related."

The following acting principles are representative of the essential principles a child will learn through the process-activity of doing drama:

1. A player's organic self is his medium of expression. A child needs to explore and discover his individual resources as he learns to express himself with control of his physical (outer) and psychological (inner) self.

2. A player learns to express and control his physical body as he moves with ease, relaxation, and a sense of form in relationship to effort, space, shape, and other players.

3. A player learns to concentrate his full attention to perceive and imagine a character, action, motive, and circumstances in relationship to a variety of sensory stimuli.

4. A player learns to concentrate his full attention to imagine a character in action in relationship to given circumstances.

5. A player learns to imagine and improvise a character's physical actions (including speaking) in relationship to the imagined circumstances.

6. A player learns to perceive and act a character's physical actions (including speaking) in relationship to the character's motive.

7. A player learns to act a character's physical actions in relationship to the character's motive and in relationship to the physical actions of another character in the circumstances which are being acted by another player.

The mode in which essential principles of each drama element are designed in the process-activity learning experiences will be illustrated as we investigate the fourth and final question: How should drama be taught to children? In discussing the content of the drama program, we have suggested some answers to this question. However, we will examine the learning-teaching process in more detail by considering briefly, first, the child as learner in drama, and second, the role and responsibilities of the teacher.

Because a child is inclined naturally to learn about life by exploring his perceptions through dramatic play, education in drama uses this natural interest. Therefore, motivation for learning is strong. Considerable experience shows, however, that motivation and interest are sustained and increased for a child when learning satisfies basic needs. In teaching drama, therefore, these factors are emphasized to satisfy a child's needs in relationship to learning drama.

1. The subject matter for drama activities in each of the four phases needs to be drawn from pupils' perceptions and imaginations and from literature, primarily from poetry and stories for younger children and stories and from scripted plays for older children who progress to Phase Four of the program.

2. Relevance in learning is important to a child, for he needs to perceive a relationship between his problems in life and what he learns in drama concerning human problems. He needs to attempt to solve, struggle with, manage, or triumph over the problems.

3. Problem solving is important to a child because he becomes involved when being challenged to identify problems and find solutions to different ones, rather than having easy answers provided for him.

4. Personal satisfaction and competence are important in a child's learning, and he needs the satisfaction and enjoyment of proving to himself in relation to others that he is increasing his ability to perceive and improvise actions by learning to concentrate and to draw on his own resources and imagination.

5. Communication is important to a child, for in drama he not only satisfies basic emotional and social needs as he communicates in discussion and improvisations but also has opportunities, as he progresses in learning, to collaborate with others in the process of communication in a performance for an audience of peers.

The role of the teacher in this view of teaching drama seems to defy exact description. It remains an individual mode which differs somewhat with each teacher. Jerome Bruner, in *The Process of Education,* offers pertinent suggestions for the teacher: "Mastery of the fundamental ideas of a field involves not only the grasping of general principles, but also the development of an attitude toward learning and inquiry, toward guessing and hunches, toward the possibility of solving problems on one's own. . . . To instill such attitudes by teaching requires something more than the mere presentation of fundamental ideas. Just what it takes to bring off such teaching is something on which a great deal of research is needed, but it would seem that an important ingredient is a sense of excitement about discovery—discovery of regularities of previously unrecognized relations and similarities between ideas, with a resulting sense of self-confidence in one's abilities."

A teacher's responsibilities in teaching drama as an art appear to be threefold:

1. To plan for the provision of adequate space and physical facilities;
2. To provide a regular schedule for teaching drama and to establish a learning environment that encourages each child to participate actively so that he becomes involved in learning experiences;
3. To develop a sequential program first, by defining goals for each phase of the child's learning, stating related goals as performance objectives, and second, by designing activities to involve the child in achieving the objectives.

To conduct an effective drama program, the teacher needs a classroom that can be turned into a workshop activity laboratory. It should be large enough both for the instructional program and for performances before an audience. The ideal drama laboratory should provide space for a playing area, for storage, and for a space that can be used as a stage with provisions for the use of stage curtains and for simple stage pieces, lighting, sound, and costume requirements; but a classroom that is approximately twenty by thirty feet will provide sufficient space for instructional activities for twenty children if the seating facilities are flexible. The minimum physical requirements for teaching drama include adequate space for twenty children to move freely and storage space for instructional aids. The teacher needs instructional aids, including a drum, a cymbal, tambourines, a record player, and a library of selected recordings. Several instructional aids are required also to teach the element of design-staging: basic lighting equipment, consisting of four portable "light trees," and an assortment of colored gelatines and frames; various textures of colored yardage to be used in teaching fundamentals of costuming; a variety of objects to be used in the construction of sound effects, including such objects as bells, horns, sandpaper, siren whistles, wooden blocks, and sound effect recordings; and stage pieces, such as step units, platforms, rectangular rises, large wooden or styrofoam blocks approximately two feet square and in various shapes and sizes, including triangles, rectangles and semi-spheres.

It is the teacher's responsibility to schedule drama classes on a regular basis. If behavioral change in a child is to occur, the child will need to participate in drama for approximately two hours each week. Scheduling of classes into appropriate time blocks should be organized in relation to other classes in the English language arts program. However, class periods should vary in length at different educational levels. Drama classes for the early elementary children will be more effective if classes are scheduled in fifteen- or twenty-minute periods daily or three days each week. On the other hand, at the upper elementary and junior high school levels, three forty-five minute class periods each week have proved more effective. Because it is necessary for each child to participate actively in each learning experience, classes ideally should be limited to not more than twenty children.

The teacher becomes the most important factor responsible for the effectiveness of the drama program. The teacher who is convinced that drama as an art can assist a child's natural development and learning will have a positive attitude toward each child and a desire to foster the development of each individual's unique personality. This attitude and his personal interest in each child will be key factors in the way in which a teacher designs problem-solving activities and guides children to experience them. The teacher will be aware of children's interests, which, in turn, should form the subject matter for children's innumerable imaginings and improvisations. He will establish a pleasant, noncritical learning environment in which each child will find security in the realization that he is respected for being himself and using his resources as he aims to solve problems for himself. Such an environment will provide each child the opportunity to concentrate, perceive, imagine, and become involved in the processes of doing drama in a calm, quiet learning atmosphere where each child becomes excited about the challenge of solving drama problems for himself.

Although a teacher will discover his own manner of asking questions and of posing problems and activities, problem solving is so basic in this view of drama that it provides a general five-step teaching procedure:

1. Orientation and presentation of the problem.
2. Discussion to guide individuals to perceive (identify and interpret) key factors of the problem.
3. Organization of children into related learning roles (players and audience) within the physical space of the room.
4. Participation by children to solve the problem and observation by the audience to observe different solutions.
5. Discussion to facilitate feedback by players and audience in response to individual behaviors used to solve the problem.

It is a teacher's responsibility to develop a curriculum that establishes a systematic order for teaching basic principles of drama to children. A curriculum is a guide that interrelates objectives, content, structure, and learning activities. As explained earlier, the drama curriculum is structured in four phases with acting serving as the central element through which basic principles of each drama element will be learned by children in active problem-solving experiences. The activities are designed in relation to a specific performance objective. A performance objective, stated in terms of what the child will do as he becomes involved in a particular activity, grows out of a basic drama principle that needs to be learned *by doing*. The child will achieve performance objectives by active participation in activities designed to teach a basic principle as it is applied in the creative process of doing drama.

The remainder of this paper aims to illustrate the employment of the curriculum. It indicates how an objective is stated in terms of a child's performance by describing the child's behavior in the process of the activity. It indicates the nature of problem-solving activities and illustrates how an activity is related to a basic principle of acting in the processes of *perception, imagination,* and *improvisation*. It illustrates also how these processes are combined in Phase One, the introductory phase of the curriculum for a child who is being introduced to the art of drama at any age level from five through eleven years.

PHASE ONE. *Perception*. Based on the acting principle related to a child's discovery of his expression in body movement: a player learns to express and control his physical body as he moves with ease, relaxation, and a sense of form in relation to effort, to space and shape, and to other players.

> *Performance Objective*. Given the task of identifying and moving a body part as it is named by the teacher, a child will move each designated part of his body by twisting, bending, or stretching it.
>
> *Activity*. Let's see if you can discover how many parts of your body you can move by bending, twisting, or

stretching as you stand in your own space in the room and listen to hear the name of a body part as I call it. Ready? Move arms, hands, fingers, wrists, elbows, shoulders, neck, head, face, mouth, eyes, nose, waist, back, spine, one leg, the knee on that leg, the ankle, the toes on that foot, the heel on the same foot, now the other leg, the knee on that leg, the ankle, the toes of the foot, the heel on this foot, the foot itself.

Performance Objective. Given the task of identifying and controlling the movement of each body part in relationship to the factor of time (fast, slow), a child will stretch a body part in slow motion as the part is named by the teacher. (This task will be followed by movement in fast motion.)

Activity. Let's see if you can control the way each part of your body moves by stretching it in slow motion as you hear each body part as I name it. (Teacher calls body parts as was done in the above activity. This activity will be followed by moving a body part in fast motion.)

Note: Performance objectives and related activities will be designed in relation to a child's extensive exploration of body movement and control until he has mastered the principle honestly although not precisely. For example, the following movement themes will be used in this phase of learning: effort factors of weight (heavy and light movement), factors of space, including the rising and sinking of the body upward and downward in space, opening and closing (broadening, contracting) the body in space and forming body shapes (arrow-like, ball-like, wall-like, screw-like).

Performance Objective. Given the task of identifying and moving in locomotion near the floor in a given space of the room the child will listen and move in relation to a locomotor movement that is named by the teacher.

Activity. Let's see how many different ways you can move yourself through the space of the room by traveling near or close to the surface of the floor as you hear me call a way for you to move. Ready? Walk. Run. Crawl. Walk. Pull. Push. Run. Walk.

Performance Objective. Given the task of identifying and moving in elevation through the given space of the room, the child will listen and move in relation to a specified movement as it is named by the teacher.

Activity. Let's see how many different ways you can move yourself through space by traveling up from the floor as you hear me call a way for you to move. Ready? Hop. Skip. Leap. Jump. Jump from one foot to the other. Jump from one foot to the same foot, from both feet to both feet, from both to one, from one to both.

Note: Each of the above movements in locomotion and elevation may be explored in relation to the effort factors, or time and weight, and open and closed body positions.

PHASE ONE. *Perception and Imagination.* Based on the acting principle: a player learns to concentrate his full attention to perceive and imagine a character in action.

Performance Objective. Given the task of perceiving and imagining a character from a body stance or position, the child will move and control ("hold") his body position until he imagines and identifies a character in action.

Activity. Let's see if you can discover how to make believe you are a person or thing different from yourself. It is something like molding a person or thing out of clay. Here, instead of using clay, you use your body and different body parts to shape your body to make believe it is a character, a person or thing different from yourself. We will start with something easy. Close your body to get into the smallest position you can. Imagine you are a tiny seed. As you listen to the sound of the drum beating from a light beat to a heavy beat, see how you may change from a little seed to the most beautiful tree you can imagine. Use your head, shoulders, arms, hands, fingers, back, spine, and legs to change into the shape of the beautiful tree you are imagining. Ready? Curl up tightly. Listen for the drum beat to help you grow and change into the shape of a beautiful, full-grown tree.

Note: Activities similar to this, based on this acting principle and concerned with this child's imagining a character in relation to body shape, may be designed from stimuli within a child's frame of reference. Activities may be similar to the following that were suggested by children: changing from a big snowy mountain to a puddle of water, growing from a drop of water to a giant ice cube, changing from a tall tree to sawdust, changing from a little snowflake to a giant snowman or snowlady, and changing from a speck of dust to the earth.

Imagining character in action activities may be designed also from the body actions of bending, shaking, stretching, twisting, twirling, opening and closing, and locomotor and elevation movements. Imaginations will be stimulated further when the child is given the task of doing any of the above actions in combination with the movement factors of weight and time.

It should be made clear also that many different kinds of stimuli other than body movements may be used in the process of guiding children to perceive and imagine character in action. Visual stimuli, particularly objects with interesting shapes, form, rhythm, or textures have proved effective. The following are examples of the kinds of objects that have stimulated children to imagine interesting characters in action: objects from nature (driftwood, gnarled root, stones, shells, kelp, flora and fauna, seed pods, fish, insects, fog, fire, water), food items (lemon drop, a biscuit, cracker, vegetables, fruits, salt, pepper), furniture (rocking chair, pillow, rug, chair, stool, table), packages (can, rectangle, square, sphere, different colored wrappings), and clothing (hats, caps, capes, aprons, shoes), including textured materials (velvet, satin, burlap, lamé).

PHASE ONE. *Perception, Imagination, Improvisation.* Based on the acting principle: a player learns to perceive, imagine, and improvise a character's physical actions in relation to the character's motive.

> *Performance Objective.* Given an imagined character in action, the child will identify a purpose (motive) for the character's action and will improvise physical actions in relation to the character's purpose
>
> *Activity.* Now we are going to see if you can bring your character to life. Suppose you think about the character you just imagined you were. If your character came alive to do whatever he was doing, see if you can imagine why he is doing what he is doing. In real life a person has a purpose for doing what he does. For example, if your character were a "bull charging through a field," ask yourself why he is charging. What does he want as he charges in this strong way? Does he want to fight another bull? Does he want to charge after a dog who has chased him? Does he want to charge after a person? What do you think is his

purpose in charging? As soon as you imagine and decide on a purpose for your character's action, see if you can make believe you are that character doing what he does to get what he wants.

PHASE ONE. *Perception, Imagination, Improvisation.* Based on the acting principle: a player learns to imagine and improvise a character's physical actions, including speaking, in relation to the character's motive.

Performance Objective. Given the task of improvising physical actions, including speaking, a child will imagine he is a given character in a conflict relationship with another character (being acted by another child). Each child in the role of his character will act to get what his character wants in relation to the other character.

Activity. Let's see if you can make believe you are a character in a place with another character where each of you acts to get what you want. You will use action and words. Suppose you choose a partner. You will be two brothers (or sisters), one older and the other younger. Decide between you who is the older and who is the younger one. The action takes place in the living room, where the younger one is watching his favorite television program. The older one comes into the room, sees the younger one watching television, and wants to get the younger one to let him watch a different program. The younger one wants to watch his favorite program so he refuses. Our problem is to see if you can act to get what your character wants while the other person acts to get what his character wants. Before you begin each one, imagine at least two different ways your character would go about trying to get what he wants while the other person is acting to get what he wants. You will talk to each other as if you were a brother (or sister) who does what he does to get what he wants. We will begin as soon as the younger one is in the living room doing what he imagines and believes the younger one would do as he watches his favorite television program.

REFERENCES

Bruner, Jerome. *The Process of Education.* Cambridge: Harvard University Press, 1962.

Fergusson, Francis. *The Idea of a Theater.* New York: Doubleday Anchor Books, 1953.

Moffett, James. *Drama: What Is Happening.* Champaign, Illinois: National Council of Teachers of English, 1967.

Roberts, Vera Mowry. *On Stage: A History of Theatre.* New York: Harper and Row, 1962.

Siks, Geraldine Brain. *Children's Literature for Dramatization: An Anthology.* New York: Harper and Row, 1964.

Ward, Winifred. *Playmaking with Children.* New York: Appleton-Century-Crofts, 1957.

On Teaching Oral Reading

JERÉ VEILLEUX

Associate Professor of Speech
Purdue University

The art of reading aloud is surprisingly complex. It would seem that oral reading should be no more difficult than silent reading; yet even the best sight readers often stumble, lose their places, mispronounce words, or phrase awkwardly and erratically. It comes as a distinct surprise to most of us to discover that we must *prepare* to read aloud. But simple preparation is not enough. The words, somehow, sound flat to our own ears; they lack the liveliness and the color which they have in our imaginations. So, painstakingly, we have to learn how to use our voices and our bodies—especially faces, eyes, and hands—to breathe vitality into the written symbols.

Despite our careful work, we often find that those to whom we read, especially children, scorn our artistry. Their attention wanders; our frustration grows. We wonder: what can be so infernally difficult about simply reading aloud?

It is with those difficulties in oral reading, for both student and teacher, that we are concerned here. It seems strange indeed to recall those not too remote times when reading aloud was a central classroom activity and even the dominant mode for the teaching of reading itself.

Today oral reading plays a relatively minor role in our elementary and junior high classes. Indeed, some of our difficulties in oral reading probably stem from our lifelong commitment to the silent reading process as our primary, almost only, experience with the written word.

Reading aloud is a valuable process; it is the link between the spoken and written word. The spoken word is a vital thing—vibrant in quality, flexible in emphasis, virtually infinite in intonation. The written word has permanence and is thus filled with potential for form and style. But even though oral reading is the link between speech and writing, it is much neglected in our schools. The causes of that neglect are historical and need not concern us here. But let me first suggest some of the serious consequences of our neglect of oral reading, and then discuss the difficulties that reading aloud poses in two classroom processes: the teacher reading to his students and the students reading to each other. Then I shall recommend some materials both for use in the classroom and for further help as you experiment with oral reading.

It has long been noted that the affection and enthusiasm for literature of some children can be suffocated by teachers. As small children, both at home and in pre-schools, many of us delight in discovering the magic of words. We played with them, made up nonsense sounds and sentences, and responded gleefully to rhymes and rhythms. For many of us, appreciation of literature came as naturally and easily as our appreciation of music and art; in our primitive way, we were true poets as well as little chanting minstrels and masters of the coloring book.

But after the first two or three years in school, our education may have progressively dampened our ardor for prose and poetry. The most difficult challenge in teaching oral reading (or oral interpretation, as it is most commonly called) on the college level is the difficulty in uncovering the student's feeling for literature, buried under some dozen years of education.

Why do some teachers so carefully and thoroughly obliterate children's love of literature? Surely not because they want to, but because they seem unconsciously to think they must if they plan to teach according to some prescribed course of study. Education is primarily a practical matter of preparing us for living, and literature (like music and art, which suffer from the same obliterating process) has little immediate practical utility. We *must*, for instance, learn to read as a skill, as a tool for mastering our other subjects, other aspects of our world. And in learning to read for that purpose, there is little time to spend or value to gain in "playing" with words. Words become serious business.

Thus we sometimes divorce the process of reading—with all its practical and necessary values—from the enjoyment of reading. Speed and comprehension are what count, not time for reflective thought and the capacity for emotional involvement. Now I am not challenging the necessity of our learning to read as a skill; our lives in this modern age virtually depend upon it, and there is no doubt that the ability to read silently rather than orally is one of our most important tools. What I am saying is that, in emphasizing those practical aspects of reading, we frequently discourage the kind of reading that is necessary for the appreciation of imaginative literature, reading as play for natural enjoyment.

In extreme cases, it is very easy to see the result of this early divorce of reading as work from reading as play. Often enough today we have college students who, in reading aloud, always pronounce *the* and *a* with long vowel sounds; it has become a habit for them, a very difficult one to break. They do not, of course, pronounce those words that way in conversation or even in formal speaking, only in oral reading. What exactly is the cause of this, I cannot say; perhaps it is an extreme result of word calling over the years as the student has been asked to read aloud; perhaps it is the result of too extreme a look-say approach in early teaching of reading. Such a habit clearly indicates that the student unconsciously makes a distinction between words as they are used in writing and as they are used in speech. He does not, then, read aloud naturally as a child would, but makes a pronunciation distinction solely on the basis of whether he receives the signal from the page or from his own ear or imagination.

So it is no wonder that adults have difficulty in reading to children; years of study and practice have convinced us that words on the printed page are somehow different from spoken words. And indeed this is often the case in a highly literate culture: the more complex our technical and scientific uses of language become, the more divergence between written and oral style. Thus a great part of the training of an adult oral reader centers on teaching him to divorce the words from the page and to treat them not as single words but as spoken thoughts.

The other major problem in teaching oral reading to adults is overcoming their inhibitions about the reading process. They must be freed from their sense of the practical meanings and functional consequences of words and must trust themselves to express those feelings for which the words are often symbols. These inhibitions result from an educational system through which we learn that our feelings exist at home or during recess, not in the classroom, and that the expression of our feelings should take logical, rather than emotional, forms.

Thus the adult oral reader faces the printed page with

two overwhelming handicaps. One, he unconsciously sees the words as neutral tools rather than as highly charged imaginative weapons. Two, he views the reading situation as "educational"; he is free to communicate ideas but not feelings. No wonder that his readings are flat, or that children, especially, soon lose interest.

Now what can be done? Literature, appealing almost naturally to most children, becomes so unnatural a predilection to others that they finally, because of their education, become incapable of either appreciating it or transmitting it. And each generation passes the problem on unsolved to the next.

Unfortunately, for our present generation of adults the problem is remedial. Some of us, despite the practicality of our education, because of or in spite of the last ditch efforts of our teachers (with *Silas Marner* in my generation, *Catcher in the Rye,* a better choice, now), eventually come to a sort of grudging appreciation for literature and a rueful awareness of what we've missed. Literary criticism seldom helps us, indeed often hurts with its emphasis on literature as an object to be dissected like a dead frog, its parts jarred and labeled. But a good course in oral interpretation, with fully half the time spent removing our fears of emotional expression and correcting our tendencies to see words as things in themselves, can help us to know literature as a live art once more.

The future is not all black. We need not perpetuate the traditional neglect of oral reading. But we must begin at the very beginning and be consistent with our children. Let us learn from them. Instead of taking their natural talent for literature and forcing it to bow entirely to the practical demands of society, we need to recognize the atrophy of our own poetic impulses and prevent it from recurring in them.

A program of oral reading in the elementary and junior high schools, if carried through bravely and consistently, can spare high school English teachers from having to *teach* literature to recalcitrant students, or for those of us who teach oral interpretation in college to have to spend most of our time uncovering natural feelings and modes of expression. I do not mean that the child should not learn to read silently, quickly, and with understanding. But we do not, in order to promote reading skill itself— and its concomitant uses as a tool for science, math, and social studies—need to deny its most obvious advantage as an oral tool for the appreciation of imaginative literature.

Like music, imaginative literature is essentially designed for the ear: word symbols on the printed page are like printed notes on a sheet of music. In *Music and Literature: A Comparison of the Arts* (Athens: The University of Georgia Press, 1948), Calvin Brown writes:

> No one mistakes the printed notes on a sheet of music for *music:* they are simply symbols which tell a performer what sounds he is to produce, and the sounds themselves are the music. Precisely the same thing holds true for literature and no illiterate would ever be guilty of this confusion. In fact, the only reason that we do not make the same error with respect to music is that we are largely musical illiterates: the symbols on a musical score mean little or nothing to us until they are translated into the sounds for which they stand. We are so accustomed to translating printed words into sounds effortlessly and without having physically to produce those sounds that we sometimes tend to forget their existence.

Precisely so: our habituation to the process of silent reading makes us deaf to the sounds. Only through oral reading can we continue to hear the "tones" of literature. And for the child, only through oral reading can the word

symbols retain their natural musical qualities and thus
lead to a continuing wonder and delight.

Let us turn to the practical difficulties in oral reading.
The child may bring to his kindergarten or first grade
classroom a natural affinity and affection for literature. He
has no reason to fear it, no motivation to dislike it. He has
already been read to, probably inadequately, by his parents; perhaps he has been read to much more effectively
by his older brother and sister; and perhaps he has experi-
mented freely for himself and among his friends with his
own poetic and prosaic gifts. In short, he probably enjoys
both hearing and making literature.

His first problem may be the teacher. Before he can
learn to read himself, he will be read to by the teacher.
Most of our elementary school teachers, products of the
vicious circle in our system, read aloud poorly. If oral
reading is to have any meaningful place in the curriculum, the teacher *must* read well, for he inevitably and
subtly becomes the student's model. What can the individual teacher, already beset by a host of other problems,
do to improve his oral reading abilities?

First, he needs to recognize that good oral reading does
not come naturally to anyone in our culture. He must
neither assume his ability nor avoid his responsibility. He
must recognize his own emotional inhibitions toward the
free expression of literature and his own inevitable tendencies toward emphasizing meanings rather than feelings. Above all, he must be open and receptive to the
possibilities of imaginative literature; he must recognize
its place in the curriculum as being closer to music and to
art than to spelling and grammar, despite the apparent
similarities among the language arts.

Second, he must choose his material for oral reading
carefully. Certainly most stories in the basal readers are

not suitable for the purpose of maintaining and enriching the child's literary experience, no matter what value they may have in increasing reading skills. The teacher must supplement the texts with truly exciting and challenging stories and poems. He must ask himself what responses his selections will likely evoke in his listeners and how the material can be used to stimulate the children's creative imaginations. For the teacher's oral reading is not an end in itself nor simply a pleasant diversion in the school day; rather, it is a motivating force for the child's continued exploration of his own mind.

Third, he must prepare. Sight reading is doomed to failure. Preparation means more than merely advance reading; it must include a working out of phrasings and the translation of punctuation marks into changes of pitch and rate. The teacher must prepare to read the material emotionally and he must prepare himself accordingly. A good textbook on oral interpretation (see the Suggested Readings) can help him to find answers to the technical questions involved.

But the *experience* of literature is something else again. He might better not read at all to his children unless he is willing to commit himself to the proposition that for the duration of the reading the experience of the literature is *all* that counts. (But not to read at all; perhaps I've gone too far. Is a poor teacher-reader better than none at all?) Each story or poem is a unique challenge; no textbook, nothing but his own creative imagination can tell the teacher what tone of voice, what gesture will meaningfully recreate any given literary experience. Good oral reading is a mystical blend of the right moment, the right story, the right children, and the right teacher's intuitive touch. Recognition of one's role as reader, careful choice and analysis of material, adequate intellectual and emotional preparation—these are all general requisites for the good teacher as a creative oral reader.

Here are four specific pitfalls which the teacher should avoid:

1. In the selection of material, the teacher should be careful to discriminate between literature that is childish and literature that is truly for children. Unfortunately, a vast proportion of the literature for children is remarkable only for its use of a small vocabulary and its exercise of an even smaller intelligence. *The Arbuthnot Anthology* (see Suggested Readings) is a remarkable exception. The teacher should not underestimate the natural sophistication of children—their willingness, for instance, to entertain the true as well as the miraculous, the unpleasant as well as the pleasant, the violent, even the macabre —and he should remember that their listening vocabularies are much broader than either their reading or speaking vocabularies.

2. In the preparation of the material, the teacher must feel free to take license with the written page. A comma is not sacred; it is only an indication of where the pitch might go and how the rate could proceed. The teacher must use the page symbols imaginatively as if they were stage directions for his performance, not be bound to them as if they represented grammatical rules. For instance, much of the poetry to be read will tend toward a sing-song effect because of the highly regular metres and rhymes which both children and children's writers so love. The teacher can either exploit the sing-song effect (as clearly intended in some poems) or he can fight against it (as he must in poems where the meaning should domi-

nate), but he must do *one or the other*. The sing-song is not the poem; the poem is his and the children's imaginative experience together.

3. In reading to small children, it is extremely important for the teacher to disassociate his adult response from the responses of the children. The child's attention span is shorter than the adult's, but his power of imagination may be stronger. Thus his need *to participate in the story immediately* is much greater. The teacher, as he reads, needs to provide the children (through questions and related diversions) with opportunities to participate actively in the literature. Far from being forbidden to interrupt the reading process, the children should be encouraged to interrupt and respond, to discuss their associations and the interesting ramifications of the literature, and to explore their reactions in all possible ways, even through drawing pictures and making up songs. It is the literary experience that counts, not just the literature.

4. The teacher must not read to the children *as if they were children*. Practical experience has shown that children will not be successfully patronized. They are more sophisticated little adults than a teacher might realize because they are quick to learn how to hide their honest responses from the teacher's potential wrath. For this part of their education at least, for the experience of literature, the teacher must meet the pupils as imaginative equals, indeed even recognize that some of their imaginative responses are freer, more natural, than his. He must not read down to them.

In fact, the teacher might very well find some clues as to how to read to his children by listening to the

best of his children read to him. For while literature
is not a different experience in kind for children and
adults, the normal small child has little natural difficulty or inhibition in performing literature, especially in kindergarten and first grade before the divorce of words as work and play has taken place.

This brings us to our second and most important point:
that oral reading must be done by the students themselves. Although the teacher is inevitably a most important model as a reader (and remains so, even to the
Shakespeare scholar citing a passage in his graduate seminar), eventually the teacher's reading performance needs
to be supplanted by the children's own developing performance capacities.

Is there any real reason, though, to develop a child's
capacities as an oral reader? Certainly no professional reason, for almost no one in our culture earns a living by
reading aloud. And while we have cited the difficulties
encountered as generations lose their natural capacities
for oral reading, surely the peripheral benefits to be
gained by becoming better parent-readers, say, are trivial
compared to all else the child must learn and the ever-
decreasing time in which to learn it. Neither simple
professional nor personal aims are enough to justify the
inclusion of student oral reading in the curriculum.

Yet I think there are at least two subtler, but very important, reasons for making a place in the curriculum for
student oral reading. It needs to be a continuous place
from the moment the child himself can begin to read until
he moves to the relatively specialized classrooms of the
secondary school.

The first of these perhaps subtle reasons is that oral
reading is a means by which the child's natural experience of literature can be kept alive and growing. As I have

said, literature for the pre-school child is simply one way he looks at life: for him, language as used in imaginative literature is no different from language as used in other more practical ways. Too, creating his own word patterns or responding to those word patterns created by others is simply the same activity to him. As he discovers his own ability to read and as he learns to use it as a tool to capture other areas of interest, two things tend to happen: one, the experience of imaginative literature becomes mostly a passive, solitary process, and two, the reading of such literature often seems to him an unnecessary activity, divorced as it is from both his work and play time.

The end result of these two events is, as we have seen, his discovery as a young adult that he has had no real experience of literature for many years. Consequently, English and speech teachers struggle to reinstate literature as a part of his daily, meaningful existence. Most of our children become nonreaders of literature not because they lack the skills but because there is no real motivation for them to continue to read. The experience of language as literature, despite its growing complexity, no longer reaps the very tangible rewards to be had from either work or play, and there is no way for children to share that experience directly and immediately with friends.

Oral reading as a continued activity in the classroom, even though the children could (but don't) read the same material silently, provides a motivation for the children to enjoy the experience of literature together, much as they can and do enjoy the admittedly more practical experiences in science and social studies. That is, oral reading would—if we truly believed imaginative literature to be as important as those other studies and not merely the idle pursuit of pleasure.

Simply providing the child with books or sending him

to the library does not create the experience we want—
even though it might seem to. No more would we expect
a child, after learning numbers, to explore the rest of the
world of mathematics all by himself. Literature becomes
as complicated an endeavor as mathematics and one no
less artful; some of us are misled by that very early experience of ours that tells us that literature is inseparable from
living. True, but living is the most complicated of all the
arts and sciences. Sending the child to the library also
doesn't work because it intensifies his passive response; he
needs, just as in science and in social studies, the interaction of stimulus and response provided through oral reading, not only the discussion of literature but the experience of it, to continue to challenge his growing aesthetic
sensibility.

So the second reason for a continuing role for oral reading in the curriculum is that, like creative dramatics, it
provides the child with a testing ground for his growing
capacity for artistic expression. Similar to the programs in
art and music, the oral reading program allows the child,
whatever his talent, a chance to develop artistic skills.
Oral reading is the most natural and common of all the
oral arts; it is the essence of good acting and is more
germane to many students' education than the continuing
development of their limited art and music skills.

How does the teacher proceed? Should all the children
read aloud? What should they read? When? What is good
reading or bad reading? How should the teacher react to
their readings?

First, the teacher should recognize that student oral
reading is an aesthetic activity. The analogy with art and
music is again apt; oral reading is a different sort of discipline from the other language arts. To carry the analogy
one step further, oral reading is to grammar and spelling

as playing the piano is to learning the scales or painting to learning to mix colors.

Since our purpose is to develop and encourage the child's artistic ability, and since those innate abilities will differ (though almost all children have a natural facility with words as opposed to that minority with natural talent for art and music), many of our questions are answered immediately. No, all children should not be forced to read aloud. There is no reliable guide to good or bad reading. There are no set rules as to how the teacher should proceed.

We believe that the experience of reading aloud has value as an activity in itself; the end result is not so important as the perpetuation of the experience both for what it does for the child vis-à-vis literature and what it does for him as a human being allowed and encouraged to give expression to his own, and others', imaginative literary impulses. The teacher must have the courage to believe in the activity of oral reading and an openness to experimentation with both the literature and his students. The first principle in the teaching of student oral reading is the principle of *freedom:* the child must be able to read what he wants to read, when (within limits, but certainly there must be regular times available) he wants to read it, and how he wants to read it.

A real help to the teacher in the early grades is that the children for the most part have no inhibitions about reading aloud. Many find it an exciting process. It is only as individual differences become apparent in the growth of reading skills that the child develops shyness. At this point the other students can be a real help. We have already mentioned that part of the difficulty in sending the child to the library is that he experiences literature alone; he has no social experience with literature. As individual differences become apparent in the classroom, the teacher can divide the class into groups, sometimes so that poor readers can all progress comfortably together and sometimes so that good readers can help the poor readers. The children will help each other in small groups, for they are essentially reading to and for each other, not for the teacher or even for something as frightening as the whole class. Indeed, such experiences would not be so frightening if we would let the child's talent for speaking and reading develop steadily and slowly among small groups of his peers rather than isolating him too soon as an individual and forcing him to test his skills alone before those who he knows include his betters.

If the first principle of teaching student oral reading is freedom for the child to explore his own imaginative linguistic capacities, the second principle is *naturalness.* Whatever techniques of expression are natural are right. It is as easy as that and as complicated. There is plenty of time later in high school and college for the student to polish his reading form. And unlike music and art, there is no artificial language involved, no scales or colors to learn; the child already knows what words essentially are and is fast learning what they can do. But he must be encouraged to innovate, to test language creatively, to let his imagination work through the oral experience of literature.

Thus there is no right way for any given student to read; or, if there is, he must discover what it is. The teacher is there to create and encourage those situations in which the child wishes to share his own literary experiences with others and in which he learns the best way he can communicate those experiences. The teacher of course can help the child by discussing and criticizing his readings; he can analyze the tensions, tones, rhythms, and patterns.

Oral Interpretation of Children's Literature (see Suggested Readings) is a manual that can provide him with the minimal critical equipment necessary for such guidance. But like creative dramatics, oral reading is a creative art, and the most valuable asset that the teacher has is his own creative self-confidence and his own creative understanding of children and of literature.

The practical questions as to the time and place for the introduction of oral reading must be left up to the teacher. There is no reason that I can see, and reading specialists agree, why oral reading should not begin as soon as the child begins to learn to read. It will not deter silent reading progress and indeed it may help it. Oral reading is easily integrated, of course, into the language arts curriculum, especially as a companion of creative writing; oral reading simply insures that some of the child's regular experience of imaginative literature is both social and oral. Certainly, if oral reading must be introduced in the later years (that is, if it is not continuous from grade one), the teacher faces problems: the child will already tend to divorce his literary experiences from his playground and classroom experiences and his inhibitions as a reader will already have begun to take hold. We can only conclude that, while oral reading programs are necessary at all levels, the earlier they are introduced the better. At any rate, once oral reading has been introduced, the program should continue from year to year, changing only as the student himself changes and as the literature increases in complexity of both form and content.

Assuming that oral reading is a continuous elementary and junior high activity, there are some suggestions I can make to the teacher, again regarding some practical, likely-to-occur problems:

1. I suggest that the teacher initiate the activity of oral reading not with poetry, as might seem the most likely choice because it is the most imaginative form, but with stories that contain substantial amounts of dialogue. Our desire is to manage the transition from speaking to reading without the development of that artificiality, stiltedness of diction, which I discussed earlier. Dialogue, especially from contemporary stories, embodies the rhythms of speech closest to the child's natural rhythms, and so, beginning with dialogue, he will then develop easily his oral reading facility so that it is as natural as his speech, which indeed it should be. More complex narrative and poetry can be attempted later.

2. There are problems of preparation and selection for the student as well as for the teacher. The student should never be asked to sight-read imaginative literature; he, as much as the teacher, needs to prepare and preferably practice in front of a small group before he reads in front of a larger one. While the selection of his material needs to be his, the teacher will naturally provide resources, as wide a range of material as possible. In most cases a class will tend to determine its own level of material. The teacher should not try to force Shakespeare on a junior high class that can understand or appreciate only light verse. But he should try to find materials for his students that will stretch their imaginations and at the same time speak to their own experience, even if it is circumscribed by poverty, racial discrimination, or cultural deprivation.

3. There is no one way to experience literature orally. The oral reading program should be designed for the sake of the children's experience with the literature,

not to satisfy the teacher's aesthetic preconceptions. If the principal should ask what is going on, the teacher can reply that he is carrying on one of man's oldest traditions; oral recitation began with Homer, and, indeed, Charles Dickens gave oral readings of his works.

The teacher should encourage the children to experiment, singly and in groups, with different ways of reading stories and poems aloud; he should use music, sound effects, properties, or costumes. The pupils should make up their own stories, adapt the stories of others, sing poems and pantomime them. They should discover what they like and don't like.

4. Choral or group reading is an excellent technique for developing a child's awareness of and sensitivity to the need for skills and techniques in oral reading. Here a group of children read poetry (primarily poetry, though not necessarily exclusively) in unison or sometimes in unison with individual voices at appropriate moments. Choral reading also has the advantage of sharply decreasing inhibition and almost eliminating fear of performance; it is a good way to make at least one bad reader sound pretty good, as part of a group anyway. The teacher should be especially careful to suggest appropriate material for choral reading. Not all material is suitable (though surprising effects can be achieved with some apparently unlikely material), and much material that is suitable is pretty poor intellectual and emotional fare.

Some special mention should be made of the possibilities of oral reading relative to the inner-city or disadvantaged child. Here we have children who have, or soon will have, fallen behind the ordinary level of achievement, often particularly in reading skills. Yet many of their oral language skills and their experiences can dramatically increase their interest in literature and can also be used to develop their overall language ability. The use of an oral approach with students who are orally sophisticated but who have problems with writing and silent reading must obviously be a help. The keys, of course, are material that motivates them (probably not the basal reader) and a classroom atmosphere that allows oral reading a status equal to that of silent reading. In such situations, many deprived children will surpass the privileged ones.

Some readers, at this point, may feel themselves hopelessly inadequate to the challenge of teaching oral reading. Perhaps they feel that since their colleagues in the lower grades failed to meet the challenge, it is probably now too late to help their students. It is never too late. The process just becomes a bit more difficult. But it never lacks for either sheer enjoyment or satisfaction. Oral reading always becomes a remarkable but unformulable amalgam of art, literature, and psychology. Even if the teacher is less than the perfect oral reader himself, he should trust to the children. He should give them the chance, and they will find the way, for oral reading is essentially play, not work.

A program of oral reading instruction, begun in the pre-school years by an imaginative and careful teacher-reader, transformed in the early school years to a program in which the students read to each other both for the experience of the literature and for their own creative and aesthetic growth, and carried forth continuously through the middle years and junior high schools, will build a solid foundation for the child's future adult experience of literature. This is no trivial goal; we always say we think literature is important, but we need to admit that many of our attempts in the past to teach it have failed miserably. Oral reading assumes that literature can only be experienced, not taught, and that the time spent in reading aloud, far from being time wasted, is time essential to the wholeness of the child's imaginative growth.

Suggested Readings

Arbuthnot, May Hill, ed. *The Arbuthnot Anthology of Children's Literature*, rev. ed. Chicago: Scott, Foresman, 1961. A large and very good anthology of literature for children containing prose and poetry suitable for all age levels. In addition, the books contain several very helpful and informative chapters relative to oral reading: "Reading Poetry to Children" (Book 1, pp. LXIII–LXIX); "Using Poetry in Verse Choirs" (Book 1, pp. lxx–lxxxiii); "Telling Stories and Reading Aloud to Children" (Book 2, pp. ii–ix); "Books and Children" (Book 3, pp. iii–vii).

Bamman, Henry A., Mildred A. Dawson, and Robert J. Whitehead. *Oral Interpretation of Children's Literature.* Dubuque: Wm. C. Brown, 1964. A paperback manual for the teacher of oral reading containing many suggestions of specific techniques and classroom activities.

Herrick, Marvin T., "The Teacher as Reader and Interpreter of Literature." *Quarterly Journal of Speech*, Vol. XLI, April, 1955, 110–113. A brief but stirring exhortation to teachers by a professor of English.

Kershner, A. G. Jr., et al., "Teaching Interpretation: Students Recall Methods of Early Leaders." *Speech Teacher*, Vol. XI, November, 1962, 290–310. Amusing and insightful reminiscences of the great teachers of "interpretive reading" (Dolman, Rarig, Dennis, Cunningham, Bassett, Woolbert, Babcock, and Parrish) by their students.

Lee, Charlotte I. *Oral Interpretation,* 3d. ed. Boston: Houghton Mifflin, 1965. A thorough and readable approach to oral interpretation; the most popular college text in the field.

On Teaching Formal Discourse

CARROLL C. ARNOLD

Professor of Speech
The Pennsylvania State University

It makes little sense to think of teaching formal spoken discourse in the elementary and junior high schools without taking into account the attitudes toward oral communication and toward formality that a child carries within him. It cannot be doubted that one such attitude is that as formalities multiply and as one confronts them without the support of peers, risks of failure also increase. Nor are children alone in holding this view. Every teacher knows that when he has to "make a speech" the obligation looms as one that will require fairly extensive preparations and culminate in riskful moments of communication with others.

I begin this essay with so obvious a point because, somewhat paradoxically, many teachers—who know from experience that to make a speech is a specially demanding and at least mildly nerveracking experience—neglect to consider that most formalized oral discourse in a classroom seems riskful to their students. And yet it is precisely the inevitable riskfulness of formalized speech that makes developing a child's capacity to cope with it very much worth attempting but difficult to do without intensifying attitudes that may, in the end, prove socially incapacitating.

All success in speaking, of whatever sort, is closely related to the speaker's attitudes toward speaking as an *act*; so before discussing goals and techniques for teaching formal oral discouse, we will do well to look again at a child's views of talk and of formality. Consider a child who has no special intellectual, environmental, or physical disadvantages. Even at six or seven he has encountered a good many pressures, especially at home and at school, toward regularizing his behavior to fit the conventions of a society he does not yet fully understand. In hundreds of ways his experience seems to say, "The world makes the rules and prescribes the forms of life, not you." Such simple things as jumping up and down or wriggling must be formalized—games and dancing will do, but unsystematic exuberance is frowned on. Asking questions is fine most of the time, but the world seems determined to use any idly curious question as a basis on which to build lessons. A simple question about a kitten can get turned into the lesson that kittens grow into cats, children into men and women, and so on and on. Everything must have a point or an outcome, whether one wants it to or not.

The world's rules provide many ways for doing basically natural things unnaturally. Behavior then becomes "proper" and "useful." Talking is certainly not excepted. Talking to hear yourself talk is out. Talk that does something for somebody or to him is generally acceptable, but many forms of so behaving are bad form or improper.

It does not take long for a child of relatively well-ordered experience to notice that many words and phrases refer to nothing but the rules of the games invented by some not-quite-identifiable "they." The words demand that things one wouldn't ordinarily do, be done. *Proper* and *improper* are such terms; so are *correct* and *incorrect, the rule is, follow the form, formal,* and many more.

Each child learns, and is expected to learn, that speech can easily be improper or incorrect. What is said, who says it, where it is said, and how it is said—all get sorted out into behaviors that fall within accepted rules and those that do not. Talk, within the adult world at least, is almost entirely form- and rule-bound activity, and a speech seems especially rule-bound. A child should certainly be excused for coming to the conclusion that making a speech is doing a thing one wouldn't do unless asked or forced to. And to a perceptive—though simplistic—child, it may also seem that nothing ever happens as the result of formal talk and speeches that wouldn't have happened better if people had sat down and had "real" talk.

I suppose few children work out their attitudes toward what the adult world calls formal discourse quite in the way I have just pretended, but some or all of these attitudes and misunderstandings can be found in any class from kindergarten through adult-education courses. To discover that twisted views of speaking are widespread, one has only to ask young children to discuss such a question as "What do you do in making a speech that you don't have to do when you are just talking?" There are few classrooms in America where it will not be learned, in answer to this question, that the chief differences between talk and a speech are that in the latter case you have to stand up, stand straight, watch your grammar with special care, speak slowly, don't look at the floor, memorize what you are going to say, and speak louder than usual.

These sincere observations reflect appalling but entirely understandable misapprehensions of what either formal or informal talk must be if a talker and listener are to experience a fully communicative relationship. The general thrust of the childhood attitudes is that form—not reason or human need—prescribes what formalized talk shall be.

It is the thesis of this essay that misapprehensions about formalized talk are neither inevitable nor irremediable. Elementary and junior high school teachers can make great contributions toward their pupils' social adjustment by structuring and treating children's experiences with formal oral communication in ways that reveal the reasonableness, normality, and social potentialities of formalized speech. To do this requires special attention to the climate of opinion toward all communicative acts in the classroom. It also requires intense awareness on the part of teachers that communication is not a thing; it is, as my colleague Gerald M. Phillips has put it, "both a process and a relationship." To prevent or to remedy disabling attitudes toward formalized speaking requires, procedurally, that *at no point* in the child's experience shall the formalities—the formal or usual features—of talk or the settings for talk be treated as significant *except in virtue of their practical usefulness to the speaker and his listeners.* Any other kind of treatment of formalization in oral communication flatly misrepresents the facts of life.

Skilled teachers have amply proved at all educational levels that to insist that forms in communication are significant only functionally is to lay the base for enhancing students' capacity to communicate orally with others at modest length and with socially valuable consequences. Building upon this premise, I shall discuss in the remainder of this essay those conditions under which the capacity to communicate effectively can be helped to grow, suggest general educational goals that can be attained through introducing formal speaking as a common classroom experience, and propose pedagogical patterns likely to make experience with formalized speech constructive rather than socially irrelevant or personally disabling.

I

A child's need for successful experiences in extended, somewhat formalized talk is twofold. American society allows few of its citizens to evade situations which demand relatively uninterrupted talk. The taciturn and the silent must compensate for their eccentricity, else society penalizes them by overlooking them, by characterizing them as socially dull, by withholding responsibilities and rewards. The demand is not for oratory; it is for cogent, coherent talk that defines and directs social action; it is for talk that gets social work done in popular ways and is a part of the democratic distribution of social responsibilities. But a child's need for experience with formalized speech is also an egocentric need. Even small children stammer in perplexed frustration, "But it's my turn to talk now; you have been talking." They only display their humanity—their need to become socially influential beings.

In the dual—individual and societal—need for humans to discourse with special responsibility and influence lies the justification for introducing formal oral discourse into the learning experiences of children in grades K through 9. Nor is formalized speech an artificial or irrelevant phenomenon in these classrooms; here, as in society at large, there is work that needs to be done through formal talk, and in most children there is human need to work somewhat systematically upon the others among whom they live. Not even the presence of silent ones belies this rather sweeping observation, for there is overwhelming evidence that reticence is little enjoyed by the reticent. They, in particular, need assistance toward accepting their social burdens and their opportunities for self-realization.

Though it is perhaps too seldom attempted in systematic fashion, it is not difficult to create within any school an educational milieu in which gradations of formality in oral communication emerge as natural, practical ways of accomplishing necessary business and of creating human relationships that students need to experience and generally enjoy. There is, especially in the earliest years of education, no need for speaking somewhat formally to seem alien to everyday life or unnaturally threatening to the self. Happily, it is upon the youngest child's ordinary experience that comprehensive programs establishing the normality of formalized communication are best and most conveniently based.

Almost no kindergarten or playground fails to ring with the formalizing of communication for the practical purpose of solving inevitable social problems and for the gratification of human needs to have social influence. The five-year-old twins who play outside my study window and the sixth-grade girls who play on the opposite side of my house daily organize themselves in something like the following way: "I want to talk to you others because I want to change what you are doing. (Usually unspoken: Also I want to feel myself a part of the tribe of influential human beings.) We can't all do entirely different things; then nobody would be together with anybody. So give me a chance to try to control you, because I think I see how we ought to run things here. I say we should . . . because. . . ." This is an adult's interpretation, of course, but it is true to one of many kinds of event that every elementary teacher observes almost daily. Children discover they must systematize communication or endure unpalatable social organization and frustration of their own aspirations. Primitively and unselfconsciously, they accordingly stage settings for formalized direction-giving, announcing, reporting, debating, and other modes of formal discourse to whose sophisticated understanding and use the educational system is committed.

Since the ordinary modes of formal discourse emerge in natural though crude forms in the social life of any child, there is no need to introduce them as artificial modes of communication operating under rules imposed by outside "they's" and "them's." The pedagogical problem is to preserve and refine the climate of pragmatism and regard for common human needs under which children formalize because they need to.

Perhaps it is now safe to state what might, without preliminaries, have seemed a subversive concept: most of the so-called forms of formal discourse do not need to be taught in the usual sense. In rudimentary fashion they have already been taught by experience; what is needed is to make their *effective* use a natural, pragmatic goal in classroom experience and in teaching.

Unfortunately, classrooms are not always ideal places in which to accomplish things in naturalistic fashion, but the right conditions can emerge; it matters little whether they develop naturally within a community of pupils or are engineered into being by an astute teacher. Thus, the capacity of a child to create and influentially communicate spoken messages of modest length and formality can be enlarged whenever:

1. The child wants to influence those with whom he can communicate in the classroom.

2. Those who listen are intellectually and emotionally prepared to let the speaker try to influence them.
3. Both the speaker and his teacher-adviser recognize that for the moments of speaking at least, what happens among the listeners is the only immediately relevant measure of the speaker's effort.

The importance of these three conditions derives from the hard fact that communication is not a thing but is a process and a relationship. Without the wish to affect others, any relationship that may develop between a talker and the rest of the world is accidental. Only the speaker who genuinely tries for control over others' perceptions is representative of real life; only he can learn the nature of communicative experience from involvement in it. Also, in moments of genuine oral communication, listeners do concede at least the possibility that they may change in consequence of what the speaker says. Without this concession, no speaker can test himself against the conditions of real-life speaking.

The third condition is sometimes more difficult to obtain in classrooms than the first two; it requires what is for some teachers a radical change in strongly established attitudes toward communicative acts. Teachers of the language arts are especially likely to prize forms and procedures over immediate effects for the understandable reason that to teach any language is to teach a code that is explicable largely on the basis of convention rather than rationality. Also, to teach literature is, among other things, to teach how an artist achieves significant expression within a form or by means of a form. In both cases form is of major significance, as it may or may not be in the human relationships present in genuinely communicative formalized talk. The distinction was aptly put by Herbert

A. Wichelns in an essay entitled "The Literary Criticism of Oratory":

> . . . poetry always is free to fulfil its own law, but the writer of rhetorical discourse [or the maker of speeches] is, in a sense, perpetually in bondage to the occasion and the audience, and in that fact we find the line of cleavage between rhetoric [including speeches] and poetic.

Speeches are attempts to do something here and now —to or for the people who hear them, not to or for someone who is elsewhere. If a talk does what it was meant to do, it succeeded at least in an immediate sense. Doctrines of form, propriety, and correctness are to this degree irrelevant in moments of spoken communication unless the people the speaker tried to influence chose to apply those doctrines. In his *On Christian Doctrine*, St. Augustine put it thus: "What profits correctness in a speech which is not followed by the listeners—when there is no reason for speaking if what is said is not understood by those on whose account we speak?"

Thus, at least for the moments of speaking, the results in the audience measure success in discourse. Full recognition of this necessary condition is sometimes difficult to maintain in classrooms because the customary hierarchy of authority must be reversed: peers judge speakers; the speaker does not preside, he solicits; and the teacher is in some sense an unrepresentative auditor, hence an irrelevancy except as observer.

I should draw attention to my repeated qualifications "in a sense" and "in some sense." Today's "success" or "failure" is not a sure measure of tomorrow's undertaking in speaking. To create the conditions for fair and honest understanding of spoken communication in a classroom, however, one must accept today's speech-induced achievements as facts about communication. One need not admire them as the highest achievements possible under the circumstances, nor believe the same effects can be made to occur again by the same strategies, nor agree that the audience with whom the effects were achieved was a profound or even a representative one.

To encourage or establish this third condition for enlarging a child's capacity to influence through formal talk requires at least three things from a teacher: (1) that he be especially clear in showing his pupils the processes and relationships that constitute oral communication in the immediate circumstances; (2) that he be candid enough to accept the fact that speaking may for understandable reasons succeed even when it violates many "forms" and "rules" which other listeners might prefer to see observed; and (3) that for doctrines of correctness he substitute doctrines of pragmatic consequences.

There is nothing mysterious or unusual about these necessities. Formal speaking acquires its significance by its effects. Every observant child knows this is true in *his* world. Let the truth be denied in the classroom and the child may play teacher's game, but the teacher's integrity is lost and his judgment on matters of communication and social relationships is unlikely to be trusted in the future.

II

In most language arts programs, the "composition strand" or "communications skills program" is conceived developmentally. As the maturing child confronts increasingly complex communicative tasks, the curriculum draws attention to comparably sophisticated communicative tools and procedures by which these tasks may be carried out. In this way a child's repertoire of resources and his sensitivity to communicative options are thought to grow as his social needs grow and his maturation allows him to understand. This kind of developmental programming suits instruction in the problems and possibilities of formalized speaking. But ought we, then, to grade the forms of speech and teach them sequentially? Shall we say that just as instruction in vocabulary, sentence structure, and the like usually proceeds from simple forms to complex forms, speech instruction ought to proceed from, perhaps, story telling in the earliest grades to extended exposition in the middle grades and to argumentation and formal debate in junior high school?

Since the American Civil War there has never been a period in which the wish to teach forms of address sequentially has not in some quarters set the patterns of instruction in written and oral English. Nonetheless, these concerns for grading the forms of oral discourse rest on assumptions that are patently false. There simply is no valid analogy between a child's familiarity with alternative forms of oral discourse and his familiarity with such uniquely literary forms as essays, sonnets, lyrics, editorials, novels, and plays. The youngest school-aged child has persuaded on many occasions, given directions, told stories, and explained. In formal discourse his need—and his older brother's—is to advance from level to level of understanding of what he has already experienced and for a gradual refinement of his maturing capacity to cope with increasingly demanding occasions.

Depth of understanding and judgment in making choices, not topics or specific kinds of skill, distinguish one level of instruction from another. In a significant article entitled "Teaching Speech to Facilitate Understanding," Professor Donald K. Smith of the University of Minnesota underscored the difference between establishing levels of understanding and specifying linguistic or other skills as primary goals in speech education. He wrote:

The key to "teaching speech skills to facilitate human understanding" seems to me simply this: that we should teach understanding of speech. The statement may seem an inconsequential juggling of word order, but it is not so intended. We should teach *understanding* of speech—not simply skill in speech—but *understanding of* speech.

It seems to me that the teaching of speech *skill simply as skill,* and the teaching of speech *skill as both a product of understanding and an avenue to understanding* require somewhat different strategies of instruction. . . .

Teaching students to understand speech comprehends and includes instruction in speaking skills, but the teaching of skills can be approached with little or no attention to an orderly acquisition of information and concepts. . . . I would not discount the central importance of skill in language instruction. But the merely skillful man dealing with a behavior as complex as speech may stand as a threat both to his own best purposes, and the highest aspirations of his society. . . . And men who simply speak effectively, but who know little of the complexities of this most significant of all behaviors represent an important instance of power without wisdom.

Smith was, of course, thinking of the whole of education, not of the early years alone. Nonetheless, his distinction between teaching specific skills for the sake of those skills and enhancing understanding of speech with a due regard for orderly, meaningful acquisition of information and concepts is as important in the elementary school and the junior high school as in the high school or college.

With what I hope is due regard for orderly acquisition of knowledge, I suggest that at least three general kinds of understanding (therefore, clusters of skills) can be set out as feasible goals for the teaching of formal oral discourse in grades K through 9. These goals are achievements one might realistically hope to find in an average ninth grade child of normal verbal ability.

1. He would understand, on the basis of repeated, realistic experiences in one-to-many communication,

that he can exercise significant social control over his peers through speech designed and presented according to his own plans.

2. He would understand, on the basis of realistic experimentation, that planning and executing any formalized speaking is an exercise in choosing strategies of influence that are appropriate to both his own intentions and the concerns of those to whom he speaks.

3. He would know as the result of study, introspection, and realistic experimentation that plainly recognizable order is a prime virtue in extended talk, and that a variety of structural and supportive procedures is available to him whenever he must make strategic decisions in preparing what he wants to say in a manner suitable to his subject matter, his purpose, and the concerns of the specific listeners he will address.

At first glance some topics usually prominent in discussions of speech education seem omitted from this list of desired attitudes and knowledge. The goals I am suggesting identify no learnings affecting the choice and use of language and none relative to the physical delivery of spoken messages. The weighting is deliberate. The body of knowledge a graduating junior high school student is presumed to possess as the result of ten years of experience with formalized speaking is knowledge of how one may organize ideas for oral communication and how one may support ideas to the satisfaction of audiences.

Centuries of pedagogical experience suggest by good example and bad that a clear, psychological separation needs to be maintained between teaching which directly seeks to improve language and speech patterns per se and that which seeks to improve and direct students' adaptation of messages to audiences. Recognizing that children and even teachers are only too prone to overvalue words and stylistic devices for themselves alone, Quintilian, in the first century A.D., cautioned in the eighth book of his *Institutes:*

> . . . as a rule the best words are essentially suggested by the subject matter and are discovered by their own intrinsic light. But today we hunt for these words as though they were always hiding themselves and striving to elude our grasp.

As though addressing stylists and sloganeers of the twentieth century, this first Imperial Professor of Rhetoric at Rome pled for commonsensically adaptive speaking, not artifice:

> . . . the anxiety devoted to the search for words, to the exercise of the critical faculty and the power of comparison is in its place while we are learning, but not when we are speaking. . . . If . . . the powers of speech have been carefully cultivated beforehand, words will yield us ready service, not merely turning up when we search for them, but dwelling in our thoughts and following them as the shadow follows the body. . . . nothing should be done for the sake of words only. , . .

A famed twentieth-century teacher of speech, James A. Winans, urged the same kind of cautious restraint in considering techniques of delivery appropriate to public speaking. In his textbook *Speech Making,* Winans wrote:

> I have considered conversational quality [in delivering public speeches] chiefly as a matter of delivery, but it goes deeper than that. Much [that determines effectiveness] depends upon what ideas are expressed, much upon how they are put into words, and very much upon how they are related to the interests, understanding, beliefs, and sentiments of those addressed. . . .

Without minimizing the importance of grammar, vocabulary development, stylistic experimentation, or development of conventional articulatory and gestural behaviors, I am proposing that teaching aimed in these directions be carried on *apart from* teaching that concentrates on helping children adapt formal discourse to the demands of audiences and situations. The reason is psychological rather than logical. Several completely natural psychological forces tend to draw children's and teachers' attention all too strongly toward those superficialities disturbing to Quintilian and Winans. These forces include the following:

1. The more formalized any speaking becomes, the more stressful it is for the speaker; hence, the more likely any speaker is to try to ease his stress by resorting to artificial behaviors and by seeking protection in observing the rules instead of working out rhetorical strategies practically suited to his relationship with his audience.

2. When any of us first perceives a new concept or pattern of experience, we are prone to mistake appearances for essences, to value formal, quickly seen characteristics of the new phenomenon above the reasons for the phenomenon's existence. For this reason, there is persistent danger that forms and obvious but relatively insignificant features of oral communication will distract a child's (and a teacher's) attention away from less obvious features of communicative acts and settings which in fact determine what judgments and behaviors are relevant and practical *in the immediate circumstances.*

3. The normal egocentricity of children makes it especially difficult for them to distinguish between purely *expressive* utterance and planned, *communicative* discourse. Accordingly, they require much assistance

if they are to perceive that *adapting* what they say to the standards of others is the only means they have of exerting influence on other people.

4. Any classroom is an artificial setting by comparison with the "real world." Most children realize this without being told; therefore, realistic communicative experiences have to be carefully planned if formalized speech of integrity is to occur.

Each of these forces, obstructive to successfully teaching formal oral discourse, is unavoidable; but each can be minimized by foresighted teaching that generates countering, practical, true-to-life forces.

III

To this point I have from time to time referred to an instructional program for teaching the processes and relationships involved in formalized speech. The emphasis on "program" has been deliberate; only a consistent attitude and instructional policy toward formal oral communication can generate the abilities and understandings I have proposed as the long-range goals for all formalized talk in any classroom. But mere consistency across ten years of education is not of the foremost importance to a program of teaching formal discourse. What has to be taught and how it may best be taught argue for programmatic teaching rather than for a series of courses or units.

What a child learns about formal talk in the first grade is not different in kind from what his brother must learn in the seventh or ninth grade. The older brother has more difficult, more complex communicative problems to solve, and he must acquire more subtle tools and skills for their solution; but at base the first grader and the ninth grader deal with the same problem: How can one best relate his ideas and himself to a particular group of others in ways that will change the others as he intended? The first grader's ideas differ from the ninth grader's. The others who are to be changed are markedly different, and the ninth grader's intentions may be far subtler than his brother's (though this is not necessarily so). Still, what the younger child has to learn about formalized talk and formally organized listeners is psychological and linguistic knowledge, which is not supplanted but is refined and amplified as he makes his way through the levels of education.

The learnings to be inculcated, sustained, and refined through a ten-year program of teaching formal, oral discourse might be stated thus:

1. Substantive learnings:
   a. Formalized speech needs to be self-evidently focused upon a theme or central thought clearly significant to one's listeners.
   b. It makes a difference to those who listen how clearly and how reasonably ideas are related to one another *by words.*
   c. There are several standard structuring systems that are familiar to most people and therefore relatively easy for them to follow. Each is capable of emphasizing some kinds of relationship and each usually minimizes others. (Ultimately we could expect the child to know that narrative structure highlights time sequences and minimizes such relationships as causation, to have a repertoire of common patterns of rhetorical organization, and to be able to choose among these according to his strategic needs.)
   d. Because speech must take listeners from where they were to where the speaker wants them to

arrive, introductory, transitional, summary, and concluding functions must be learned and their strategic possibilities for formal discourse discovered and used. (The familiar lore on organizing speeches, on methods and types of transitional materials, and perhaps on methods of emphasis constitute the content to be progressively amplified and refined from grade to grade.)

e. The different ways of building sentences and of ordering words within sentences produce different effects on listeners. (The practical consequences of previously taught grammatical structures become speech content and at the same time reinforce grammatical learnings.)

f. Information can perform various supportive functions when offered to listeners as proof or clarification. (The functions of examples, testimonies, statistics, visual aids, and possibly elementary logic and theory of persuasion are the substance of teaching at appropriate levels.)

g. Speaking *as action* offers a wide variety of resources for describing, emphasizing, and proving. (The uses of descriptive gestures and movements, the emphatic functions of movement, vocal inflection, loudness, and rate, and the nature of visible cues to sincerity and authority all become content to be learned in this connection.)

2. Attitudes to be learned:

a. The primary problem in composing a speech is to choose and use ideas, words, and behaviors that are at one and the same time strategically adapted to one's purpose and to one's listeners' willingness to believe.

b. Audiences think and feel much like individuals to whom one talks informally; therefore, to make a speech is only to devise and carry on an enlarged conversation with others.

c. Listeners' judgments of any talk are to be taken more seriously than the judgments of anyone else —including the speaker and his teacher.

d. Since listeners cannot listen as carefully or understand as fully as readers read, speakers have to be clearer, fuller, yet simpler than they would need to be in some kinds of writing.

e. The only reliable answer to what one should do or how he should do it in formalized speaking is *proceed in whatever ways will accomplish your purpose with this audience under the particular circumstances* in which you talk to them.

Many less important facts and learnable attitudes are, of course, subsumed under these primary, cognitive, and attitudinal learnings.

Whenever students speak formally in show-and-tell, in reporting on field trips, in reviewing books, in reporting decisions of small groups, or in any other connection, these seven substantive learnings and five attitudes ought to predetermine the situations under which the speaking will occur, how speaking assignments or invitations to speak are issued, what kinds of assistance the teacher will give each pupil as he prepares, and how both teacher and students respond to and evaluate the speaking that results. The kinds of learning that are to be the outcomes of experience in speaking formally do not alter from grade to grade nor does the general character of teaching. The subject is always the same: understanding formal speech as process and relationship and learning its uses under progressively more sophisticated circumstances.

What I propose in the listed learnings and attitudes amounts to a syllabus—a teacher's agenda—directing all pedagogy whenever and wherever formalized speaking occurs in any classroom in grades K through 9. The agenda is stable, but as children change and as the circumstances for speaking alter, the substantive knowledge they must be helped to learn becomes increasingly detailed. The attitudes to be inculcated remain the same for all age groups; they are steadily reinforced by the gradually enlarged understanding that listeners are always the problem and the judges. Aristotle pointed to this ancient truth in the fourth century B.C. The "problem" and the "judges" of formalized speech in an American classroom remain as they were in the Athenian agora, for the relationships involved in effective speaking derive from the nature of humankind.

Plainly, to teach formal oral discourse in the earlier years of education requires a program of instruction consistent from classroom to classroom. Its implementation is less difficult than might at first appear. Instruction in formal speech may be integrated with other teaching, or it may be independent of other teaching; alternation of the two patterns as opportunities dictate is ideal.

There is an apparent but actually unreal paradox in thinking of direct instruction in formalized speaking and at the same time thinking of "genuine" speaking that seeks to influence others realistically in the classroom. At least three approaches to speech instruction resolve the paradox with marked success: a communications laboratory approach to formal discourse, a classroom community approach, and a communicative tools approach. These methods of teaching are not mutually exclusive, and it is easy to shift from one approach to another; only the teacher need know which she is using in a given moment.

The communications laboratory attack can be directed toward problems of formalized speaking whenever any class can be motivated to consider a problem like "How can we tell stories better?" or "What makes directions confusing?" Whenever there is readiness to notice a particular feature of spoken communication, experiments can be undertaken to explore that feature or solve the problem. In the earliest grades, poorly told stories and confusing directions or explanations can be deliberately (and joyously) concocted and their faults as communications thereby studied. A boring story once built by a class, can then become raw material for repeated attempts to substitute interesting and colorful features for the boring ones and can provide the opportunity for experiments in improving the tale by changing styles of delivery or language. The same approach to more sophisticated structural and stylistic problems is constantly possible in later years when presenting better argument, devising explanations of foolproof clarity, or building a genuinely amusing monologue from basic jokes are set as problems to be attacked and solved by students' experimentation. To become the excuse for genuine practice in communicating orally, an aspect of speaking formally need only be made to seem a matter worth testing.

The topics and problems which the communications laboratory method can accomodate are almost unlimited, and, of course, they go far beyond matters relating specifically to formal discourse. Central to the method—insofar as formal speech is the subject of concern—is genuine understanding among pupils and teacher that discovering how to solve difficulties of formal talk is, for the time being, even more important than making a polished talk.

Under these circumstances, talks are not genuine attempts to exert social control now; they are genuine attempts to practice what social control through extended speech requires in the real world. I have heard one teacher using the laboratory approach set the climate thus: "As soon as one of us leaves this classroom, mistakes in talking cost us. Here we can make mistakes free, and then help each other to avoid such mistakes when we go outside." The statement fairly represents the spirit and the motivational groundings of the laboratory approach to teaching speech.

The laboratory approach in teaching is in part an attempt to circumvent the artificiality of a classroom as an arena for social control through formal discourse. It is also a procedure calculated to forestall development of such attitudes toward oral communication as the supervisor of language arts in the elementary schools of a small industrial city in Pennsylvania described in these words: "Somewhere between the third and sixth grades, a majority of our students, including many of the very brightest, seem to conclude that it's safer not to try to talk seriously in school than it is to run the risk of making a mistake or 'being wrong.'" In a communications laboratory, the risks of being wrong are low and mistakes become occasions for learning.

The classroom community approach to teaching oral communication and numerous other subjects is familiar under one name or another to all teachers. A special project is undertaken, a club is formed, or representatives are delegated to gather information for an entire class. Reports, statements of opposing or supplementary ideas, extended characterizations or descriptions, even parliamentary debates become necessary social acts in order that the community's work may be done. Speech, including formal speeches, becomes socially necessary, and opportunities for formalized discourse naturally and normally multiply. That kind of social control becomes a need of the community and its members.

The possibilities for formal speaking that arise from community enterprises in classrooms are too familiar to require enumeration. There will be speaking, but it is sometimes forgotten that mere verbalization yields no necessary increment of understanding about or skill in oral communication. Unless direct teaching is introduced before and after a child carries out a speaking responsibility in his community, any growth in his capacities will have been accidental.

Happily, both preparation for formal speaking and review of speaking can be realistically and educatively emphasized within the framework of larger classroom projects. Speeches and reports are prepared by committee in real life; why not in the classroom? Speech consultants are employed by industries, churches, politicians, and professional organizations. The same role is realistic for a teacher. Post mortems of political and advertising campaigns and of speeches are commonplace in the real world. Why not in a classroom, whenever formalized speech has been used socially? Almost every classroom project offers opportunity for systematic planning of related communications programs and for evaluating those programs once they have been completed. At both points there can be valuable new learning (and new teaching) of what is required to influence socially through speeches of modest length. Whether the opportunities will be used depends only on whether teachers choose to teach the requirements of *effective* talk when they choose to provide opportunities for talk.

What I have called a communicative tools approach is

a traditional approach to speech education. It is the pattern of instruction in which tasks and activities involved in communicating orally are singled out and taught as topics for special study. Teaching may focus on the several steps of preparing a speech, on the different forms and types of speech, on forms of supporting material, on stylistic features of language, and on aspects of delivery. Because much of the teaching in elementary schools is integrative, not focusing upon subjects per se, the tools approach to teaching formal discourse is most appropriate to early instruction if used in combination with one or both of the approaches I have already described. There are good reasons for analyzing communication and for examining in detail the tools and options open to communicators as the tools approach does; but one may doubt that even junior high school students love abstractions (e.g., distinguishing reasoning from evidence, identifying figures of speech, studying the abstract relationship of movement to emphasis) or learn most swiftly and thoroughly when concepts and topics they do not yet need are the objects of their attention.

Identifying the tools of communication and exploring their theoretical possibilities as these tools become needed seems the wisest pedagogy in elementary and junior high schools. Basic tools are always needed; it is the need to penetrate their potentialities that varies. Order and reasons why are active concepts and persistent problems even to children in kindergarten. At least some theoretical concepts of logic are needed and are intelligible to junior high school students. It is, then, both feasible and reasonable to build *toward* conceptualizations of tools and principles used in formal discourse. By gradually introducing and refining rhetorical tools as they become relevant, the communicative tools approach can adapt to the childrens' educational needs rather than arbitrarily impose adults' conceptual schemes for which children may or may not be ready.

Whether a classroom is, in a given moment, a communications laboratory or a community engrossed in carrying on its business, each instant of awareness that "we have to make a choice in order to communicate as we wish" is an instant in which direct teaching about communicative tools becomes relevant and constructive. Shall a group's representative "tell all we did" or "tell one thing we saw"? In so simple a problem lies a need to distinguish the communicative possibilities of narrative from those of description. The first or second grade child who realizes that some of his peers' stories seem too long has made a discovery that gives opportunity for teaching a rudimentary version of the concept of feedback in communication: by watching listeners, a story teller can estimate their interest and adjust such things as length according to what he observes.

Across the years of K–9 experience, alert and rhetorically informed teachers will find ample opportunity to enlarge and perfect their students' awareness of what formalized spoken communication consistently requires and what total repertoire of ordering and supporting procedures they may choose from in accomplishing their objectives in formal relationships with audiences. In the last analysis, a graduating junior high school student's ability to conceptualize and generalize concerning the power of speech will reflect the wisdom and rhetorical knowledge that his teachers, since kindergarten, have set before him as from time to time he stood alone with his ideas, risking failure, but working for success in establishing an honestly influential relationship with others.

IV

The syllable form in "formal discourse" tempts. We see recurring ways of carrying out the processes of communication. We name the ways we think we see. These are the forms we know—just patterns we have seen before. In a classroom it is easiest to teach the names of things and their descriptions. Hence, the litany of forms of discourse: informative speaking and writing, persuasion and argumentation, debate, problem-solving discussion, entertaining speaking or writing, lecturing, and the like. But at base, speaking is simply soliloquy, display, or communication. The forms are only consequences of the relationships we try to establish by means of speech. Forms of speaking are abstractions evolved after observing the artifacts of once-live communicative relationships. They are of secondary, not primary, concern in serious study of oral communication; but because it is easy to name and define, there is always the temptation to teach the forms but not the substance of anything as complicated as oral communication.

It is the burden of this essay that children's naïve perceptions of communicative acts and their reasons for being furnish an ample, primary, true base on which to ground programmatic teaching that will culminate in the awareness of the potential of communicative speaking, whatever its formal characteristics. At the very least, such instruction in grades K through 9 can produce ninth graders who possess enabling attitudes toward formalized speaking and the systematic knowledge of how ordering and supporting ideas function to alter human relationships.

On Finding Something to Say

EDWARD B. JENKINSON

Director, English Curriculum Study Center
Indiana University

and

DONALD A. SEYBOLD

Assistant Director, English Curriculum Study Center
Indiana University

EDITOR'S NOTE When a teacher asks pupils to write a theme or give a speech, he is likely to hear this chorus: "What am I going to talk (or write) about? I don't have anything to say." The familiar refrain stems from the fact that pupils have not been taught how to find something to say rather than from the fact that they actually do not have something to say.

The following steps that help pupils find "something to say" are based on the process described in chapter two in *Writing as a Process of Discovery: Some Structured Theme Assignments for Grades Five Through Twelve* by Edward B. Jenkinson and Donald A. Seybold (Bloomington: Indiana University Press, 1970). This process for finding material and words for themes was tested in more than fifty schools, and teachers in grades five through nine discovered that the process could be modified slightly to help pupils discover how to gather material for speeches as well as for themes.

Given the instruction to "talk about something you know," a pupil might put together several sentences about his parents, his hobby, his pet, or his pet peeve. Instead of spending some time thinking about the subject for his speech, he will probably say the first and most obvious things that come to mind if he has not been taught (1) how to examine a subject, (2) how to gather information about it, and (3) how to analyze it in terms of both his purpose for speaking and his audience.

The tasks that follow are designed to (1) help a student learn how to ask questions about his topic so that he will discover what he knows and does not know about it; (2) help him sift through the answers to the questions, deciding which are pertinent for both his purpose and his audience; (3) help him find precise words for effective communication with his listeners; and (4) help him order his information appropriately to achieve his purpose and to communicate with his readers.

The first two tasks give the pupil an opportunity to talk about two things he thinks that he knows well. First, he is asked to give a subjective description of his neighborhood. Second, he is asked to give a subjective description of something in his neighborhood that he finds appealing or unappealing. For each task he is given both specific purposes and a specific audience.

Speech 1

Speech task: The pupil is to examine the block or farm on which he lives, or the housing project or community in which he lives, paying particular attention to those things and/or people that make him like or dislike his neighborhood. Then he is to describe his neighborhood in such a way that his listeners, people his own age, can tell immediately why the speaker likes or dislikes it. As the pupil examines his neighborhood, he should concentrate on those features he can use to make a listener his own age feel the same way about the neighborhood as the speaker does. Furthermore, the speaker's task is to learn how to select and use words that will affect his listener and stimulate a desired emotional response.

Purposes: The speaker's purposes are to express his feelings about his neighborhood and try to persuade listeners his own age, through choice of words and details, to react to the neighborhood in much the same manner as the speaker does.

As the teacher, your purposes are (1) to help pupils learn how to gather information for their speeches, (2) to help them understand what speaking to a specific audience means, and (3) to help them learn how to choose words that stimulate emotional responses in their listeners.

Step 1. *Finding information to include in the speech and choosing precise words that will stimulate an emotional response in the listener.* You should devote several class periods to this particular step in order to show pupils how to gather information by helping them to learn how to ask questions and to choose the specific words with which to convey that information. You also need to spend some additional time, particularly with this first assignment, explaining to pupils what it means to give a speech to a specific audience and how they go about it.

We hope that a pupil will always realize that whatever he says may be subjected to rigid analysis by the audience he is addressing. Whether he is writing a letter, a theme, a short story, or giving a speech, whatever he says or writes will be criticized by his speaker or reader—particularly if he fails to communicate. The pupil should realize that criticism of what he says does not have to be spoken or written; the lack of response on the part of a reader or listener may sometimes be the most devastating criticism that the pupil will ever receive. This lack of response may indicate that the reader or listener did not understand the message, or was bored by it or by the way it was written or spoken, or was completely disinterested in the topic. The criticism of writing and speaking is frequently unspoken or unwritten, and a pupil must be made aware of that. For example, if a pupil writes a letter to a friend requesting that the friend perform a specific task, the writer may consider that he communicated well and that the request is a reasonable one if his friend actually performs the task. If the friend does not, the writer needs to reexamine both his request to make certain that it is reasonable and the letter to make certain that it is comprehensible.

The speaker who understands the implications of an audience will make certain through his choice of words and details that his audience understands what he says, or at least he will make every attempt to help his audience understand his message. The awareness of audience is vital if a writer or speaker is to discover what he knows or does not know about his subject, his language, and himself. Therefore, it is important that every pupil realizes that he is trying to affect an audience. And he must be aware of his goal both during the discussion of an assignment and during the actual writing or preparation for his speech. As he gathers information for his theme or speech, the pupil should never lose sight of his purpose—to present information in such a manner and in such precise words that his audience will react to his neighborhood in some specific way.

Immediately after explaining this first task to your pupils and after discussing with them what speaking to a specific audience means, you should tell them that the audience for this speech is a group of pupils their own age who do not live in their community. Each pupil should understand that his purpose is not to please his listeners or you, the ultimate judge of the speech, but to express his feelings in such a manner that his listeners will feel approximately the same way about the neighborhood as the speaker does.

Pupils should discuss the problems and possibilities inherent in speaking to an audience their own age. They will probably consider the use of slang. You should not discourage such use in this particular speech, but you need to point out that some slang words and expressions have particular meanings only in a limited area. Therefore, a pupil might not communicate with a listener who does not live in his community if he employs slang words and phrases that are not widely used. You might have several pupils write current slang words or expressions on the chalkboard and then ask each pupil to write on a piece of paper what each of the words or expressions means to him. By discussing the many meanings that will probably be given to some of the words, you can help pupils conclude that the overuse of slang may block communication with a listener even when he is the same age as the speaker.

Every pupil in the class knows that you will be the final evaluator of his speech. But you should make it very clear that he is not speaking to satisfy you or speaking to please you in any way. Instead, he should be free to tell his listener, a person his own age, exactly what he feels about the area in which he lives, and he should try to express his feelings in words that will make his listener feel approximately the same way about the neighborhood as the speaker does.

A pupil should never feel that he is speaking simply to please a teacher. We believe that preparing a speech or writing a theme should be a process of discovery. In that process, the speaker or writer should learn what he knows or does not know about his subject, his use of language, and his audience. He should always write or speak honestly to express himself, not to please someone else, unless that is his avowed purpose. Pupils at all levels of instruction tend to think that whenever they get a poor grade on a theme or a speech they have not yet caught on to what the teacher wants, or they do not know what the teacher likes. A pupil will never be able to explore his world honestly in writing if he thinks that his job is to write or say only those things that please his teacher. Instead, he should always feel that he is addressing an audience and that his purpose is to communicate with that audience exactly what he knows about a subject or what he thinks or feels about it.

After a pupil has firmly in mind the fact that he is writing for a pupil his own age who lives in a different community, he is ready to begin the process of asking questions about his subject so that he can gather information to include in his speech. By taking pupils through a search for significant questions—the kinds of questions writers ask in order to discover what is relevant in their experiences—you can help pupils learn how to find material that is appropriate to the purpose of the task and to the audience. The importance of the search for material through questioning cannot be stressed too much, for the pupil who does not learn how to question, how to probe, will probably treat most subjects only superficially.

For this particular task, the first questions that pupils ask might include some of those listed below. We suggest that you write several of those questions on the chalkboard before you ask pupils to propose additional questions, which should also be written on the chalkboard. You will want to encourage pupils to ask as many questions as possible, helping them analyze the questions to determine whether they are relevant in terms of the purpose of this task and the audience. You will also want to help them group the questions in related categories. By grouping them carefully, you can help them structure their papers. For example, if the pupils were to ask the questions below, adding additional questions that stem from the answers to the first ones, they could put their answers together in an order that would give the speech structure.

1. What is special about my block, farm, housing project, or community: What, if anything, makes it different from other blocks, farms, housing projects, or communities?
    a. Do the kinds of buildings or the arrangement of buildings make it different from other neighborhoods? Or do the buildings and the arrangement of them make it look just like any other neighborhood in the area?
    b. Are there any yards, trees, or flowers? Are the lawns well manicured? Are the yards big enough for children to play in?
    c. How can I describe the buildings and the arrangement of them so that my listeners will either like or dislike my neighborhood?

2. Is my neighborhood attractive because the houses or buildings are maintained well by the owners, or is it unattractive because it is old and run-down?
   a. If the houses or buildings are kept in a state of good repair, how can I describe this condition to my listeners so that they will find the block attractive?
   b. If the neighborhood is "old and run-down," what words can I use to describe the run-down condition instead of simply writing that the block is "old and run-down"? What does old and run-down mean?
   c. Do I find my neighborhood attractive or unattractive because all the houses or apartments look alike? How can I best persuade my listeners that the similarities of the structures make the neighborhood or community attractive or unattractive?
3. What things in my neighborhood do I find appealing or unappealing?
   a. Why do I find them appealing or unappealing?
   b. What words come to mind when I think of those things or when I see them?
   c. What do those things look like?
   d. What words can I use to help my listeners picture those things?
4. What colors in my neighborhood make the block appealing or unappealing?
   a. Why do I find them appealing or unappealing?
   b. What words can I use to help my listeners picture those colors?
   c. If paint is peeling off some of the buildings, or if stains on buildings make them unattractive, how can I best describe such conditions to my reader?
5. What odors in my neighborhood make it a pleasant or unpleasant place in which to live?

    a. Will my listeners want to visit my neighborhood if I tell them that it "smells good"? If not, how can I best describe the odors? Are words like *fragrant* and *smells good* sufficient?

    b. If I find my neighborhood unpleasant because it "stinks," do I need to tell my listeners more to persuade them that it is an unpleasant place because it "stinks"? What words can I use to persuade my listeners that the odors are unpleasant?

    c. To help my listeners smell those odors that are either pleasant or unpleasant, can I compare them with the odor of gardenias, or baking bread, or stale garlic, or rotting fish, if such comparisons are appropriate?

    d. If the odors are difficult for me to describe, can I help my listeners smell the odors by describing the source, such as a pizza parlor, rows of flowers, overloaded garbage cans, or the putrid smoke from nearby factories?

6. What kinds of people live in my neighborhood? Do they help make it a pleasant or unpleasant place in which to live? If the people in my neighborhood do not behave like people in other neighborhoods, should I describe some of their actions so that my listeners will understand why the people make the neighborhood pleasant or unpleasant? Is it sufficient to tell my listeners only that the people are friendly or unfriendly?

7. How much should I tell my listeners?

    a. What must they know about my neighborhood to make them like it or dislike it?

    b. Should I tell them everything about my neighborhood, or should I tell them only enough to make them feel the same way I do?

8. How should I begin my speech?
    a. Is it sufficient to begin simply by saying that "My block is great" (or "My block stinks")?
    b. Do such statements excite my interest when I hear them? If they do not excite me, will they excite a listener?
    c. Is there a better way of getting started than by simply saying "My block is great"? If so, how should I begin my speech?

As we have already noted, you should encourage pupils to ask as many questions as they can to help them find information and precise words to include in their speeches. You should also encourage pupils to challenge the questions that their classmates pose during this discussion, urging them to ask themselves if each question will yield an answer that is appropriate to the purpose of this particular task. You should further encourage students to enter into a dialogue in which they consider the use of such words as *good, exciting,* and *great,* and the effect that such words have on an audience.

As pupils search for precise words to answer the questions they posed in class discussion, you might want to discuss with them the various shades of meanings that words have for different persons. You might do this, for instance, by having pupils discuss what kinds of things they consider exciting. By eliciting many answers from, say, collecting stamps to watching a horror movie, you should be able to help them conclude that a word like *exciting* is used so frequently to describe so many different kinds of things and activities that the word, itself, will probably not persuade a listener that the thing being described is truly exciting. Other words or phrases or use of details will probably need to be substituted for the word *exciting* to persuade a listener that the thing being described is actually exciting.

Through class discussion, then, each pupil should begin to understand that simply calling a block *beautiful* or *dirty* to show that he does or does not like it is not enough to persuade his listener that the block is pleasant or unpleasant. Instead, if he dislikes his neighborhood, he needs to pick out those objects which make him dislike it and describe them for his audience. He might also show why life is tolerable or intolerable on the block by describing some of the actions of his neighbors. In his description, he will want to use words that will make his reader either approve or disapprove of the actions of the neighbors. You need to emphasize to your pupils that a speaker must select from all those things that are either appealing or unappealing and describe them in such a convincing manner that their audience will respond in the manner that the speaker wants them to.

We have already noted that, as pupils pose questions, you should help them decide which are pertinent and which are not. By so doing, you can help pupils avoid the inclusion of extraneous material in their speeches, and you can further help them order the information while they are posing questions and considering the choice of words with which to answer those questions. For example, you might ask pupils how they plan to begin their descriptions if they like their neighborhoods. If several pupils like their neighborhoods because of the many trees and the new houses and the people, you might ask them which of those things makes the neighborhood most pleasant. Then you might suggest that they begin with a description of the most pleasant thing and move on from there. Or they may want to begin with a summary of the things on the block that make it pleasant. But regardless how they begin, they must always bear in mind that they should arrange the material primarily for the benefit of a listener, not for themselves, and they should further arrange it in an order that will make the greatest impression on a listener. During the discussion of the arrangement of material, you should encourage pupils to suggest several arrangements and also to argue with one another about the merits of the arrangements. But the arguments should always center on the effectiveness of the arrangement for a listener, not for personal reasons.

Again, we stress the importance of free and prolonged discussion (so long as it is lively and fruitful) of the problem of finding information and precise words. We are convinced that pupils need all the help they can receive from both their teachers and from one another; and pilot-school teachers have assured us that class time is very well spent when they take several class periods for the initial speeches or themes in this sequence (or for the first writing assignments or speeches a teacher might give from any part of this sequence) to help pupils pose questions, discuss answers, select words, and consider ways of arranging their answers.

Step 2. *The assignment.* After you have completed the discussion on finding information and precise words, we believe that you should repeat the assignment task, purpose, and audience so that every pupil will know exactly what is expected of him. A pupil who is ready to prepare a speech should have all of these things clearly in mind:

1. that his task is to examine his neighborhood carefully, concentrating on those things that he finds either appealing or unappealing;
2. that he is to select only those details that will help him persuade his listener, a student his own age who

does not love in his neighborhood, that his neighborhood is pleasant or unpleasant;
3. that he is to describe his neighborhood in such a manner that his listener, too, will find the neighborhood either pleasant or unpleasant;
4. that he is to use words that will cause his listener to react emotionally to the neighborhood.

Speech 2

Speech task: The pupil is to select some object in his neighborhood, in his home, in the city, or in the school that he likes or dislikes intensely. He is to select an object or place—not a person—that causes him to react emotionally to it. His emotional response may be one of standing for several minutes admiring the object, or it may be that he tries to avoid the object because it disgusts him. After selecting the object or place, he is to describe it in such a manner as to cause his listener (in this case, the teacher) to react in the same manner as the writer does.

(Several pilot-school teachers reported that some of their pupils chose to describe their bedrooms, or a particular business establishment in their community, or a favorite hangout. Some pupils described trees, paintings, trinkets, and even articles of clothing. The pupil should feel absolutely free to select any object or place for this speech just so long as it is one that causes him to react emotionally whenever he sees it.)

Purposes: The speaker's purposes are to express his feelings about a particular object or place and try to persuade his listener, through choice of words and details, to react to that object or place in much the same manner as the speaker does.

As the teacher, your purposes are (1) to continue helping pupils learn how to gather information for their themes, (2) to continue helping them understand what speaking to a specific audience means and what triggering an emotional response in an audience requires from the speaker, and (3) to continue helping them learn how to choose words that stimulate emotional responses in an audience.

Step 1. *Finding information to include in the speech and choosing precise words to convey that information and affect an emotional response to it.* After each pupil has selected an object that pleases or displeases him, you should give the class sufficient time to consider the problem of posing questions and searching for precise words with which to answer those questions. Before pupils begin asking questions and selecting precise words, they should be told that you are the specific audience for this speech even though the entire class will be listening. You might want to discuss with them again what speaking to a specific audience means, and you might also make clear that pupils are writing to communicate with you—not to please you.

For this assignment, some of the questions that were suggested for Speech 1 will also yield appropriate information. But other questions need to be asked, and pupils should consider, in class discussion, a number of them. Here are just a few that you might want to suggest if pupils do not pose them first:

1. Why do I like or dislike the object that I selected?
   a. What about it pleases or displeases me?
   b. Are there particular colors that please or displease me?

    c. Are there particular odors that please or displease me?

    d. What words can I use to convey to the listener why the particular colors please or displease me, and what words can I use to convey to the listener that the odors please or displease me?

    e. Does the shape of the object please or displease me? If so, why?

    f. What is the shape of the object? What words can I use to describe it?

2. How do I feel every time I see the object?

    a. How can I express that feeling to a listener?

    b. Is it sufficient to tell the listener that the object is beautiful or ugly or pleasing or unpleasing, or must I describe it more adequately to get him to feel the same way about the object as I do?

3. Can I honestly say what there is about the object that pleases or displeases me intensely, or do I like or dislike it so much that I cannot analyze it objectively?

    a. If I cannot look at the thing objectively to determine why I like or dislike it so intensely, can I find words forceful enough to convey my intense emotions to the reader?

    b. When I reexamine the object to try to determine why I respond to it in a particular manner, can I look at it without becoming emotional?

Those last three questions are difficult for junior high or upper elementary pupils to answer if they are not considered carefully in class discussion. We pose such questions because we have learned that the major danger in this assignment is the tendency for a pupil to overreact to the object being described. Many pupils tended to think that hyperbole is necessary to get a listener to respond the way they wanted him to. As a result of this tendency to over-react or use hyperbole excessively, many of the themes or speeches were false, or stilted, or mushy. Your problem here is to help pupils avoid romanticizing their observations so much as to make them unbelievable, and perhaps even embarrassing to the listener.

To show pupils how the overuse of hyperbole might make a listener distrust a speaker, you might select an advertisement that makes excessive claims for a product. As pupils analyze the advertisement, you might ask them which words they doubt. Does the soap, for example, make clothes the whitest white ever? Will the deodorant guarantee that the young lady will catch her man and lead him to the altar? Is the advertisement copy believable? If not, why not? Has the advertising copywriter overstated his case? Has he made so many claims that the reader begins doubting him and the product? Why do pupils believe that the writer used the words that he did and why did he make so many claims? What was his purpose? Did he achieve his purpose if the students tend to doubt what he says?

The point to be made here is that the pupil must always be honest with himself and with his audience if he intends to persuade his listener to feel the same way about any object as he does. He cannot overstate his feelings. He cannot attribute to an object qualities that it does not have. Nor should he attribute to himself emotional responses that he does not honestly make. In other words, he must always "tell it like it is" if he plans to persuade his audience.

This is one of the fundamental problems in communication. Many writers, politicians, teachers, religious leaders, labor leaders, and businessmen tend to overstate their case. As a result, we tend to disbelieve what they say.

Some people can persuade us to act the way they want us to through exaggeration, excessive claims, hyperbole, and effusive language; others fail. They fail because they push us to the point that we can no longer believe what they say.

The problem here is to help the pupil avoid making excessive claims about the object he is describing, to help him avoid using language that is not believable, and to help him understand that even though he is attempting to trigger an emotional response in his listener, he must always be honest with himself and with the object he is describing.

The pupil should understand that once his listener begins asking, "Does he really expect me to believe that?" he has probably caused the listener to react in just the opposite way that the speaker intended.

Step 2. *The assignment.* The pupil who is ready to prepare his speech should have all these things clearly in mind:

1. that his task is to describe an object or place that he either likes or dislikes intensely;
2. that he is to use words that will make his listener (the teacher) feel the same way about the object as he does;
3. that he is to avoid using words like good, bad, pretty, or ugly, but instead to describe the object in such a manner that the listener will consider the object as being good, bad, pretty, or ugly.